HORRIBLE HISTORIES

AWFUL
EGYPTIANS

Terry Deary Illustrated by **Martin Brown**

■SCHOLASTIC

In fond memory of Rosemary Bromley, 1922–2005, without whom
Horrible Histories would not have been written. TD

Scholastic Children's Books,
Euston House, 24 Eversholt Street,
London NW1 1DB, UK

A division of Scholastic Ltd
London ~ New York ~ Toronto ~ Sydney ~ Auckland
Mexico City ~ New Delhi ~ Hong Kong

First published in the UK by Scholastic Ltd, 2006
This edition published by Scholastic Ltd, 2016

Text © Terry Deary, 2006
Cover illustration © Martin Brown, 2006, 2016
Inside illustrations based on work by Martin Brown © Mike Phillips, 2006

ISBN 978 1407 16382 6

Printed and bound by CPI Group (UK) Ltd, Croydon, CR0 4YY

2 4 6 8 10 9 7 5 3

www.scholastic.co.uk

CONTENTS

Introduction 5

Awful Egyptian timeline 7

Phunny pharaohs 10

Potty pyramids 32

Mad mummies 44

Mad mummies quiz 56

The truth about Tutankhamun 60

Cruel crime time 71

Rotten religion 84

Killing ... and curing 93

Woeful workers 99

Awful army 107

Quick Egyptian quiz 114

Cool Cleo 118

Epilogue 126

Grisly Quiz 129

Interesting Index 139

Introduction

The people of Ancient Egypt could be pretty horrible.

They just did not like the idea of dying and simply vanishing. They wanted to think there is a life after death. And to make sure they made it to that life, they had to stop their bodies going rotten.

I CAN'T ENJOY ME DINNER IF ME HAND DROPS OFF AND ME TEETH DROP OUT, CAN I?

Rich people could afford to have their bodies cleaned up and wrapped up to stop them going 'off' – a bit like when we put baked beans into a tin. The dead rich were turned into 'mummies'.

Of course, if you are going to take your body with you into the afterlife then you'll need all the things you had in this world: food, clothes, treasure and furniture.

The horrible bit was that some of the old kings wanted to take their servants and pets with them.

YOU CAN'T EXPECT A KING TO COOK AND CLEAN, CAN YOU?

So where would they find a pile of dead servants to take with them?

You wouldn't. There were no scrap-yards for dead second-hand servants. So they took LIVE servants and murdered them. Then they dropped them into the tomb with the dead king.

They did the same to poor palace pussy cats – they smacked them over the head and didn't paws to think about it.

This is the sort of foul fact that will give you nightmares. The terrifying tales in this book will haunt you like the curse of a mummy.

You do NOT want to hear what the Egyptians were REALLY like. Oh, no, you don't.

Oh very well. Here is the horrible history of those awesome ancients. Read it and see how lucky you are to be alive today, and not in evil Egypt...

6

Awful Egyptian timeline

The Egyptians are so-o-o very ancient that we don't really know where they came from. You could go on looking for answers till you're as old as a mummy (or as old as YOUR mummy).

But we do know that prehistoric people roamed around in North Africa, finding food. Then those people started to settle down next to the River Nile because it flooded regularly and made the land rich for growing crops.

Here is a rough timeline of what happened.

5500 BC Awesome Egyptian people begin to settle beside the River Nile. But they haven't invented the wheel yet – which is a bit of a drag!

3000 BC North and South Egypt unite under one king (or pharaoh), the start of a long line of rulers who will later build massive pyramids. The first pharaoh is known simply as 'Scorpion' – did he have a poison tale to tell? We don't know.

3000 BC Egyptian people invent writing around the same time as the Sumerians. Not only can we record history, we can have schools and history tests!

2650 BC The first pyramids are built in Egypt. You can see the point – it's there on the top. Pharaoh Djoser gets his people to build the 'Step'

pyramid. These pharaohs are now 'gods' who will look after Egypt and its people.

1650 BC The Hyksos from Asia invade Egypt and take over the north. Where are those pharaoh gods when you need them?

1570 BC The Kushites from Sudan attack Egypt, but their king is killed.

1540 BC Egypt switches to burying its kings in tombs cut into rock. The grave robbers were breaking into those pyramids too easily.

750 BC The Kushites attack Egypt again. This time they win and they rule for 100 years. Those gods must have been on holiday at the time…

663 BC The Assyrians invade Egypt. You can't blame them – Egypt has been attacking Assyria for centuries. Assyrian King Ashurbanipal is a great but cruel ruler. He is driven out after 20 years.

539 BC The powerful Persians conquer Babylon then go on to take over Egypt. The Persians become ancient top dogs.

356 BC Alexander the Great is born in Macedonia, north of Greece. He will grow up to conquer Persia, Mesopotamia and Egypt from about 305 BC as part of his plan to take

over the world. The Greeks will rule for 300 years, making the peasants poorer and the royals richer.

30 BC The last Greek queen of Egypt, Cleopatra, kills herself and the Romans take over the country.

Phunny pharaohs

Around 5500 BC the awesome Egyptians moved into the land by the River Nile. Every year the river flooded and left lovely squidgy mud covering the fields for a few miles on either side – lovely squidgy mud that was good for growing crops.

The people of the Nile could usually grow enough food to live on – but they were always worried that one year the Nile would let them down and they'd all starve. So they invented gods and prayed that the gods would make the Nile flood.

Then along came some really clever people who said…

These really clever people became known as 'pharaohs' – probably because they had a 'fair-old' life with peasants slaving for them![1]

Top ten pharaohs

No one knows where the pharaohs came from. Maybe they were just the leaders of peasant tribes. But around 3150 BC one became so powerful that he was more than a head-man – he was a 'king' (or pharaoh).

In school you are all in little tribes called 'classes' with a leader called a 'teacher'. But how does one teacher get to rule all the other teachers and become a 'head'?

1 Nah, that's not true. 'Pharaoh' is the Egyptian word for 'Great House'. The peasants didn't dare speak the name of their king so they called him 'The Great House', which is a bit like a Brit calling the queen 'Mrs Buckingham Palace' or an American calling the president 'Mr White House'.

Some people say…

Hmmmm! That may be true for head teachers, but probably not for the pharaohs.

We don't know a lot about the early pharaohs, but there are a few bits of horrible history we have discovered about their powerful pasts.

Your teacher may even be able to pick up a few tips on how to be a head!

Here is a top ten of phoul pharaohs…

1 Narmer (ruled around 3150 BC)

Name means: 'The striking catfish'

How did he get to be pharaoh? By being super-cruel.

Pictures of Narmer show him holding a prisoner on the end of a rope … and the rope has been pushed through a hole in the prisoner's nose. Ouch. Who knows how Narmer got his power?

There are also pictures of his enemies lying on the ground – have they just nodded off? No, because they're headless – sort of noddle off.

But remember there were no sharp steel swords or axes in Egypt. Having your head cut off with a soft copper blade would be slower and more painful than a quick chop.

2 Djoser (ruled 2668–2649 BC)

Name means: 'Holy one'

Djoser built the first of the great pyramids then he died and was made into a mummy. His insides were packed into containers called canopic jars – one each for his liver, his stomach, his guts and his lungs. That's what happened to all mummies.

But Djoser was king of South Egypt and North Egypt. To keep the people in both parts of the country happy he had to be buried in two different tombs. His body was entombed in the north, and his canopic jars had their own temple 100 metres to the south.

He was buried with food to take to the afterlife, but imagine what would have happened when his spirit got hungry...

He'd have to go for a spooky stroll to the south temple, pick up his stomach, slap it back in, then go back to the north temple for his grub. When he'd finished he'd have to drop his stomach off at the south temple and … oh, you get the idea.

Imagine sitting down to your school dinner then realizing you have to cross the school playing fields and back to get your guts.

3 Khufu (ruled 2589–2566 BC)

Name means: 'He protects me'

Khufu has the biggest pyramid, the biggest statue and the biggest ships in Egypt.

After Khufu's death his son had two ships buried beside his great pyramid at Giza. The ships were found in 30-metre pits. The ships were over 40 metres long.

'Hang on!' I hear you cry. 'Hang onnnnn a minute!'

Of course there is a simple answer. The ships were taken apart before they were buried. What was found was a sort of ship kit pit[2].

The spirit of the ship would carry the spirit of Khufu to the afterlife. Of course we don't know why they were buried a few years after Khufu … or why there were two of them.

2 Try saying that with a mouth full of marshmallows. Bet you can't – even without the marshmallows.

4 Pepi II (ruled 2278–2184 or 2218)

Name means: 'Ka of Ra is powerful'

No one can agree how long Pepi II ruled. Some say sixty years, some say ninety, but most agree that he came to the throne when he was only six years old.

Was he interested in war? No.

Was he interested in pyramids and statues? No.

Did Pepi want a puppy? No.

He was only interested in getting a dwarf for his palace.

His army set off into Africa and reports came back that they had captured a pygmy. Little Pepi was wetting himself with excitement. He wrote a message to his general telling him how to treat the captured pygmy.

Come north to my palace once. My majesty wants to see this dwarf more than all the other treasures of Africa. Take great care when he is on the deck of the boat. Make sure he does not fall over the side. When he is asleep check him TEN times every night to make sure no harm comes to him.

The pygmy got there safely. Pepi was happy.

The one thing that bothered Pepi was flies. How did he deal with the problem? Here's how…

Clever Pepi.

But Pepi lived TOO long. Some say he lived to be a hundred years old.

Egypt needed a powerful ruler, not a wrinklie. Egypt almost fell apart when he died as princes fought for the throne.

5 Mentuhotep I (ruled 2060–2010 BC)

Name means: 'The god of war is satisfied'
After all the trouble Pepi II left behind, along came Mentuhotep. He sorted out the rebels by killing them.

So many soldiers died in Mentuhotep's battles that they invented the world's first war cemetery.

In the 1920s the American historian Herbert Winlock discovered a graveyard with sixty of Mentuhotep's soldiers. Soldiers had always been buried on the battlefield where they died, but these men had all been brought back from Nubia, hundreds of miles to the south. They were buried near the tomb of Mentuhotep who had sent them to die for him.

But who got the job of bringing back the sixty bodies? In the hot Egyptian sun they would have gone off very quickly and started to smell.

PHEW! MORE FLIES THAN A PEPI SLAVE

6 Senusret III (ruled 1870–1831 BC)

Name means: 'Man of goddess Wosret'
Just south of Egypt was Nubia. The people there were a problem from time to time. They enjoyed attacking Egypt and trying to steal its treasures.

Pharaoh Senusret III wrote down the way he dealt with them:

I SHOW NO MERCY. IF YOU ATTACK A NUBIAN HE WILL RUN AWAY. BUT IF YOU RUN AWAY HE WILL ATTACK YOU. THE NUBIANS ARE WRETCHES AND COWARDS. I KIDNAPPED THEIR WOMEN, I CARRIED OFF THEIR FRIENDS, I CUT OFF THEIR WATER, I KILLED THEIR BULLS, I CUT THEIR CORN AND BURNED IT

Nice man. The message is clear – don't mess with Senusret.

But Senusret was two metres tall. His methods may not have worked if he'd only been one metre tall.

7 Tao I (ruled around 1560 BC)

Name means: 'road, pathway'

Around 1650 BC the Hyksos people from Asia invaded Egypt and took over the north. The Egyptians went on ruling in the south.

The Hyksos won their battles because they had new weapons that the Egyptians had never seen – chariots and archers with bows and arrows.

The Hyksos leader Apepi I lived in Avaris in the north. He wrote a very odd letter to the Egyptian leader Tao at Thebes in the south.

It sounds as if he was trying to wind him up…

> *I am angry, Tao. I cannot sleep at night in Avaris. Why not? Because I am disturbed by the roaring of the hippos at Thebes. I want you to do something about this at once – or else!*

Avaris is 500 MILES from Thebes.

Sadly we don't know what Tao's reply was. But if Apapi was trying to start a fight then he succeeded.

Tao and his Egyptians rose up against the Hyksos. In time they would drive the Hyksos out of Egypt …. but Tao didn't live to see it.

19

His mummy was discovered at Deir el-Bahari in 1881. The skull showed terrible wounds...

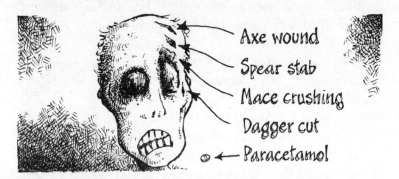

Axe wound
Spear stab
Mace crushing
Dagger cut
← Paracetamol

But the wounds were not the sort Tao would have got if he had been standing up and fighting – he was lying on his right side.

Was he knocked down and hacked? Or was he murdered in his sleep?

AND I'LL NEVER KNOW EITHER!

We'll never know.

8 Hatshepsut (ruled 1479–1457 BC)

Name means: 'Distinguished woman'

Hatshepsut was a bit odd because he was a actually a she – one of the few ancient Egyptian woman pharaohs. Pharaoh Tuthmosis III was supposed to rule, but he was only a child when his father died, so his bossy step-mother, Hatshepsut, helped him[3].

In the end she also helped herself – to the throne. She called herself pharaoh and did all the things that pharaohs did...

3 She was also his auntie – those royal ancients married anyone they took a fancy to – even members of their own family!

Hatshepsut decided that her father, Pharaoh Tuthmosis I, had wanted her to succeed to the throne. Carvings have been found in temples…

And she had the carvings changed to say…

She also changed carvings so they said SHE had driven out the invading Hyksos when really it had been her father. Power had definitely gone to her head…

Of course it couldn't last. Little Tuthmosis grew up to hate his step-mother. She died … and Tuthmosis may have had something to do with it.

NOT ME! SHE WAS CARVING UP A BOILED BABOON AND THE KNIFE SLIPPED. HONEST!

9 Tuthmosis III (ruled 1479–1425 BC)

Name means: 'Born of the God Thoth'

Tuthmosis officially came to the throne in 1479 BC, but he spent 22 years being ruled by his step-mother. So when he got the throne he tried to prove that he wasn't really such a wimp. He had stories carved in temples that said things like…

'I have killed seven lions and twelve wild bulls all by myself'

He also enjoyed killing elephants to get their ivory tusks. In one hunt he apparently killed 120 elephants[4].

But it took him twenty years to kill one step-mother.

10 Ramesses II – The Great (ruled 1279–1212 BC)

Name means: 'Re has finished him'

This 'great' warrior king made Egypt rich by invading other countries and stealing their treasures. But not all his victories were so great.

His biggest enemies were the Hittites. They were always attacking Egypt so Ramesses set off with a massive army to smash them once and for all.

He captured two spies and tortured them. They said…

THE HITTITE ARMY IS A HUNDRED MILES AWAY

JAB JAB

Ramesses thought this was his chance to attack the Hittite city of Kadesh. It was almost impossible to capture because it was on an island.

Then he discovered that the spy had lied. The Hittite army was waiting for him in Kadesh – he'd walked into a trap.

Ramesses battled bravely to save his life but when he realized he was being beaten he made peace and went home. He then had the story of the Battle of Kadesh carved on temple walls.

---

4 One of his soldiers, Amenemhab, wrote that he chopped off the trunk of a live elephant while the Pharaoh watched. Tuthmosis rewarded him with three sets of clothes.

What story did they tell?

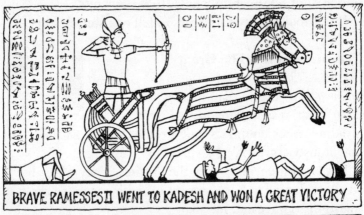

BRAVE RAMESSES II WENT TO KADESH AND WON A GREAT VICTORY

HE KILLED LOTS OF HITTITES WITH HIS OWN HAND

Er … a bit of a fib, your majesty[5]?

The pictures show how the Egyptians counted the enemy dead. They would lop a hand off each one and take them home to count them. That way a body could not be counted twice. The Egyptians knew how to do these things – you have to hand it to them.

5 The Hittites made their own carvings that gave their side of the story. The Hittites said Ramesses was the one who asked for peace. Who do YOU believe?

Did you know…?

In 1435 BC Pharaoh Tuthmosis III planned an attack on the city of Kadesh. He lined up his horses outside the city and the Hittite army did an odd thing. They sent out a mare to scare the Egyptians.

Why? Because the Egyptians were riding male horses. The sight of a female horse would send them charging off after her. The soldier Amenemhab boasted about what happened next…

That must have made the Egyptian horses a bit sad.

Bible bashing

The Hittites weren't Ramesses' only enemy. The Hebrews (Jews) suffered his brutal bullying. The Bible tells their story.

Ramesses made the Hebrews his slaves and forced them to build new temples and palaces for him. The Hebrew leader, Moses, begged Ramesses to set them free.

He tried ten times but Ramesses wouldn't budge. So God made the rivers run with blood as a punishment. Fish died, Egyptians couldn't drink, the river smelled rotten.

Then, in each Egyptian family, the oldest child died suddenly in the night. Ramesses changed his mind...

The Hebrews headed home ... then Ramesses changed his mind AGAIN. He sent an army after the Hebrews.

They caught up with the slaves at 'the Sea of Reeds'. Then God helped the Hebrews again. He made a path through the sea for Moses and his people. When the Egyptian army tried to follow, God let the waters rush back and they were all drowned.

Of course Ramesses did NOT have this exciting story carved on the walls of his temples.

That's Ramesses the Great for you – great robber, great fibber, great loser.

The phunniest pharaoh phellers

The pharaohs ruled for almost 3,000 years so there were bound to be a few odd ones among all that lot. If there had been newspapers around in those days the headlines would have been horrible. If any had survived, they'd be a bit crumbly by now and key words would be missing. Can you replace them?

The following words fit the gaps: granny's hair, money, goose, murder, elephants, magician, lion, hippo, grandfather, Greek. But which goes where?

1 HORROR! IS TUTANKHAMUN VICTIM OF ——— ?

2 SHOCK! TUTANKHAMUN'S WIDOW, PRINCESS ANKHESENAMUN, MARRIES ——— !

3 ASTONISHING! TUTANKHAMUN BURIED WITH A LUMP OF HIS ——— !

4 Wonder! HAIR CLIP FOUND BY ——— !

5 AMAZING! PHARAOH'S ENTERTAINER PUTS HEAD BACK ON ——— !

6 SENSATION! HOR AHA IS CARRIED OFF BY A ——— !

7 ASTOUNDING! KING RAMESSES II FACES ENEMY ARMY WITH JUST THE HELP OF A ——— !

8 Wow! Thutmose III escapes being killed by ——— !

9 DEPLORABLE! PSAMMETICHUS HOLDS OFF SCYTHIAN INVASION WITH MASS OF ——— !

10 EGYPTIAN SHAME! QUEEN CLEOPATRA IS A ——— .

Answers:

1 murder – some people believe the young Pharaoh was murdered by his own uncle, Ay, who went on to take the throne. But in 2005 the mummy was given an x-ray. Tutankhamun's leg was broken and that is probably what led to his death. Murder is a better story.

2 grandfather – When Ay saw Tutankhamun die he decided the best way to get the throne was to marry his widow, Ankhesenamun. She tried to run off with a foreign prince but that didn't work. In the end she was forced to marry her grandad.

DON'T THINK OF ME AS YOUR GRANDPA, THINK OF ME AS YOUR DARLING HUBBY-CHOPS

3 granny's hair – Tutankhamun was buried with a lump of his granny's hair in his coffin. No one knows why, but maybe he was fond of his mummy's mummy.

4 magician – Pharaoh Sneferu's wife lost her hair clip in a lake as she rowed across it. Sneferu ordered his court magician to find it. It was reported that the magician folded the lake in half and walked across to the clip. Oh, yeah? And there are fairies at the bottom on my garden.

5 goose – the pharaohs had all sorts of court entertainers. The one who appeared to remove the heads of geese and put them back on was obviously a clever trickster. But could he do anything with your Christmas turkey?

6 hippo – Pharaoh Hor Aha died when he was carried off by a hippopotamus. This probably served him right because he was out hippo hunting at the time. It was kill or be killed for the hippo.

7 lion – Ramesses faced the Hittite army with just his pet lion as backup. Then his friends turned up and attacked the Hittites from behind. Ramesses (and the lion) were saved.

IF I SAID I WAS LOOKING FORWARD TO THIS, I'D BE LION

8 elephants – Thutmose III was a great Pharaoh who defeated all Egypt's enemies. But he had a few close shaves with death along the way. In Syria he was almost trampled to death by a herd of wild elephants.

9 money – By 630 BC Egypt was past its best. Enemies weren't defeated, they were bribed. And – big mistake – the Greeks were paid to come to Egypt to help with the fighting. A bit like inviting a fox into your hen house.

10 Greek – Cleopatra is probably the most famous Egyptian queen … except she wasn't an Egyptian queen. She ruled after Egypt was conquered by the Greeks. She was the seventh queen of that name.

Potty pyramids

The pyramids were built as tombs for the pharaohs after they left this life. They were H–U–G–E and were filled with goodies so the kings would be as rich in the next life as they had been in this life.

History teachers have been telling us about Ancient Egypt and its pyramids since, well, since the days of Ancient Egypt. But there are some 'facts' they may have got wrong. Here are a few you might have heard...

1. Pyramid pain
Each one of the great pyramids took 100,000 slaves twenty years to build.

Who said that? A Greek visitor, called Herodotus. Old H was the world's first historian and a bit of a storyteller. You can't believe everything he said.

In ancient times he had TWO names...

HERODOTUS – THE FATHER OF HISTORY

HERODOTUS – THE FATHER OF LIES

When it came to facts about Egypt he was 'Herodotus – the father of mistakes'.

He asked the Egyptians...

Herodotus's mistake was to BELIEVE them! The Egyptians were just showing off.

The *Horrible Histories* truth is…

- Each pyramid was built by around 25,000 men.
- The pharaoh did not have 100,000 slaves in the whole of Egypt.
- They were free men, not slaves – they even went on strike when their pay was late.
- They were well fed with beef and ale – there was a fish factory and a bakery to keep them fed.
- They probably took just five years to build one pyramid.

But historians believed Herodotus and copied his mistake in their books. The mistake was repeated for thousands of years. Some school books today STILL give Herodotus' version of events.

2. Silly slopes

Some history books say: 'The Egyptians built a ramp up the side of the pyramid so they could drag the stones up to the top.'

The trouble is that a ramp of clay, mud, stones and bricks would crumble when a 16-tonne stone was dragged up it.

And another teeny problem is that the ramp would have to be many miles long ... and it would take longer to build than the pyramid.

Other history books say the Egyptians may have built a ramp that went round the growing pyramid like a corkscrew. But that takes just as much building and is just as crumbly. The *Horrible Histories* truth is ... nobody really knows how the pyramids were built.

In the 1980s a British builder came up with a clever suggestion: maybe the Egyptians used wooden jacks that lifted the blocks up one step at a time. Teams of men could work very quickly. They could finish the whole job in thirteen years and it would cost about £300 million in today's money.

It's a clever idea, and it could work, but remember the *Horrible Histories* truth ... nobody really knows.

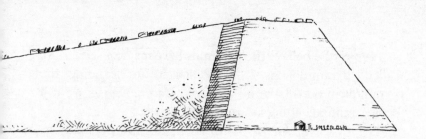

3. Pyramidiots

Some history books will tell you that the Egyptians were great at maths – even better than your teacher.

Here's why they think the Egyptians were such brainy boffins…

THE EGYPTIANS KNEW THERE WERE NOT 365 DAYS IN THE YEAR – THERE ARE 365·242 DAYS IN THE YEAR!

THEY BUILT THIS MAGICAL NUMBER INTO THEIR PYRAMIDS. THEY USED THE SACRED CUBIT – AROUND 25 INCHES

WALK AROUND THE GREAT PYRAMIDS AND YOU WILL WALK 365·242 SACRED CUBITS – ONE FOR EACH DAY OF THE YEAR

AMAZING!

People who believe the pyramids have magical secrets are called 'pyramidologists'. They started investigating the pyramids in the 1850s and modern pyramidologists are still selling millions of books around the world.

The *Horrible Histories* truth is … they are pyramidiots. The pyramids don't measure 365.242 sacred cubits. The pyramidiots didn't check their facts – they are as potty as the people who say…

THE PYRAMIDS WERE BUILT BY ALIENS FROM OUTER SPACE!

4. Boney's battering

Some history books say that near the great pyramids at Giza the Egyptians built a massive stone monster. It is 72 metres long and 20 metres tall. It has the body of a lion and the head of a man. The Greek name for it is 'The Sphinx'.

These books go on to explain that a French army, led by Napoleon Bonaparte, landed in Egypt in 1798. The French took one look at the great ugly face and decided to use it for target practice. They blasted off its nose.

No, it's not funny having your nose picked on.

The *Horrible Histories* truth is … the French army did NOT destroy the sphinx's face. It was wrecked 500 years before they arrived. A report said:

In 1318 the Arab tribes were led by Mohammed Sa'im al-Dahr – he caused terrible injuries to the head of the Sphinx.
Then, in the 1700s Mamaluk soldiers from Egypt turned their guns on the statue.

In 1737 the artist Frederick Norden drew pictures of the Sphinx with no nose – over 30 years before Napoleon Bonaparte was born.

So don't blame Boney.

Quick quiz

The word 'sphinx' means...?

a) mangler?
b) strangler?
c) stranger?

Answer: b) 'Strangler' was the name given by the Greeks to a creature that had the head of a woman, the body of a lion and the wings of a bird.

In Egypt, there are quite a few sphinxes, usually with the head of a king wearing a head-dress and the body of a lion. There are also sphinxes with ram's heads.

The famous Great Sphinx at Giza, the one with no nose, was probably carved around 2500 BC. Its face may have been the face of the Pharaoh Khafre.

Did you know...?

It wasn't only tourists who thought the Sphinx was a mighty mystery. The Ancient Egyptians worshipped it as a god.

Egyptian Prince Tuthmosis IV even saw the Sphinx in a dream. In 1400 BC he was having a nap between the Sphinx's paws. He dreamed that the Sphinx begged him to rescue it from the Sahara sands that were swallowing it.

Tuthmosis said the Sphinx spoke to him in the dream...

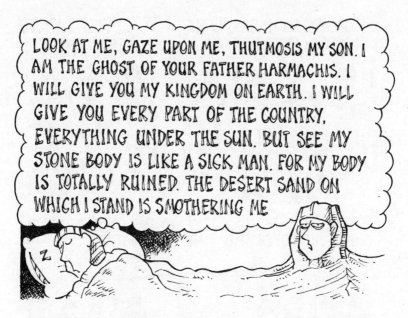

LOOK AT ME, GAZE UPON ME, THUTMOSIS MY SON. I AM THE GHOST OF YOUR FATHER HARMACHIS. I WILL GIVE YOU MY KINGDOM ON EARTH. I WILL GIVE YOU EVERY PART OF THE COUNTRY, EVERYTHING UNDER THE SUN. BUT SEE MY STONE BODY IS LIKE A SICK MAN. FOR MY BODY IS TOTALLY RUINED. THE DESERT SAND ON WHICH I STAND IS SMOTHERING ME

Did Tuthmosis dig his dad out of the sand? Of course he did.

The pyramids time forgot

Egypt has about one hundred pyramids.

But in Sudan, the country next door to Egypt, there are three times as many.

In ancient times the land was known as Kush. In 1650 BC the chieftains from Kush attacked Egypt. Their king was captured, killed and dangled from the mast of his own boat.

But the Kush were back in Egypt again in 770 BC and this time they beat the Egyptians in battle and ruled the country for the next hundred years. Then they went back home to Kush and kept on building pyramids long after the Egyptians had stopped.

The Kush also had some nasty habits – like human sacrifice. When a king in Kush died his ministers would…

① GATHER SIX WIVES AND SIX SLAVES OR PRISONERS OF WAR

② MARCH THEM TO THE TEMPLE

③ LINE THEM UP AND SMASH THEM OVER THE HEAD

④ LAY THE CORPSES OUT IN NEAT ROWS IN THE PYRAMID

Weird or what? The wives and slaves were supposed to serve the Kush king in the next life.

Just so he wouldn't get lonely they also killed dogs, camels and horses to bury with him.

There are 24 horses buried near the pyramids of Kurru in present-day Sudan. These were probably the horses that pulled the royal chariots. When King Piye[6] died they were killed so they could pull his chariots in the afterlife, as he soared through the heavens.

6 Say the word Piye like 'pie'. Many of his people kept sheep so he was really the first ever shepherds' Piye.

It's a rotten thing to do to the harmless horses. But King Piye loved horses.

There is a stone in Piye's tomb with a carved story. It shows Piye marching into a town he had just conquered. He found that the horses there were being badly treated and said…

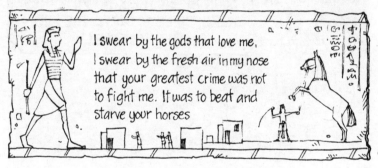

Anyway, it was believed that the ghosts of Kush kings all had wings – they could fly through the afterlife like a great bird. They didn't need dead horses to pull the chariots.

The deadly domes

Some of the biggest Kush mysteries lie in the dome tombs. These were huge mounds of earth made before the Kush had pyramids.

In the heart of the dome was a long corridor. It led to the king, who lay on a golden bed surrounded by his treasure.

There were also side passages all the way along that main corridor. And in every side passage there were dead men – lined up head to toe.

These passages were discovered in 1913. Historians said...

Wrong!

Modern tests have shown that most of the corpses belonged to the king's relations. This is a bit like your grandad dying and you being killed and buried with him. So what were they doing there?

And there's another mystery. How did they die? There are no marks on the skeletons that show they had been brutally battered.

POISON?

Possibly. But the question is, did they drink the poison themselves – suicide? Or was it forced down them – murder?

IT'S A HORRIBLE HISTORY MYSTERY

Did you know...?

In the Kush city of Musawwarat the temple has huge ramps and corridors. The walls are carved with pictures of elephants.

Why did they need such huge passageways? To march elephants along, of course. This temple could have been where they trained their fighting elephants. It must have been a bit like driving a tank.

They then sold them to the Egyptians to use in wars.

ARMS FAIR

IT IS *THE* VERY LATEST MULTI-FUNCTION-SMART-TECHNOLOGY-WEAPON-DELIVERY-SYSTEM

WHO ME?

Mad mummies

The Ancient Egyptians believed that one day the world would end. When this happened, they thought that everyone who had a body would move on to a wonderful afterlife. But if your body rotted away, you couldn't live in the afterlife. The Egyptians felt it was their duty to make sure that their dead pharaohs didn't rot. So they turned them into mummies.

A. Rip open the front of the body and take out the liver, the stomach, the intestines and the lungs - but leave the heart inside

B. Throw the brain away and pack the skull with 'natron' a sort of salt that stops bodies rotting

C. Stuff the empty body with rags to give it the right shape, then sew it up

D. Take the body to the 'beautiful house' - that's an open-ended tent in the fresh air so the disgusting smell is blown away

E. Wash the liver, the stomach, the intestines and lungs in wine and place them in their own sealed containers - canopic jars

Could YOU make a mummy? Below is an explanation of how to mummify a body. Unfortunately the instructions have been scrambled by a mummy's curse. Can you rearrange them?

(*Horrible Histories* note: If you get this completely right then you are an expert mummifier – or 'embalmer' as they were known. You can go out and practise on a favourite dead teacher if you like!)

F. Put the body on a wooden table with bars of wood (not a solid top) so you can reach underneath to bandage it

G. Perform the ceremony of 'opening the mouth'- or the mummy won't be able to eat, drink or speak in the next life

I. Wrap the body in bandages from head to toe

H. Soak the body in natron for seventy days till it is well pickled

J. Remove the brain by pushing a chisel up the nose to break through then hook the brain out with a piece of wire

I'M LOSING MY MIND

Did you get them right? Now...

Make a mask that looks like the Pharaoh when he was alive and cover it with gold. Pop him in a stone coffin, stick him in his pyramid and have a party.

Everyone's invited – except the mummy of course.

Mummy makers

Some history books say that the Egyptians were experts at making mummies from the time of the very first pharaohs.

The *Horrible Histories* truth is ... it took them 1,500 years to become experts. In the meantime they made some horribly disgusting mistakes. The first mummies were just wrapped in bandages and they turned rotten...

Who taught the undertakers to make a better mummy? The cooks! They knew how to stop a dead animal going rotten – throw away the insides and cover the rest in salt.

The messy mummifiers then found that the fingernails and toenails dropped off after the salt had shrunk the hands and feet, so they learned to tie them on with thread.

Some clumsy undertakers found the dried-out bodies went as brittle as a twig and bits snapped off them.

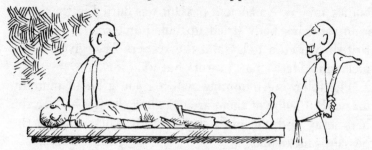

To solve the problem they rubbed oil into the dried-out corpse.

The gutted kings were stuffed with linen – but sometimes the embalmers used a bag of sawdust or moss. The arms, legs and face still looked skinny and ugly and that was no way to travel to the afterlife. So the mummifiers...

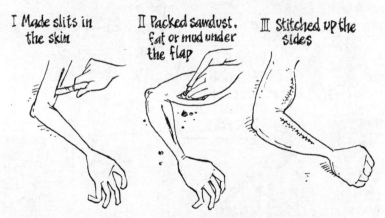

I Made slits in the skin

II Packed sawdust, fat or mud under the flap

III Stitched up the sides

But some clumsy undertakers tried to pack in too much and the corpse burst open.

Messy!

And you thought the Egyptians were experts?

Mummy magic

Of course desert-dry Egyptian summers dry up and preserve bodies anyway. An ancient peasant was buried in the desert sands and his body dried up but didn't rot. He's in the British Museum today and the keepers have given him a nickname. Here's how to work out what it is…

The following mummies will tell you a bit of mummy magic. But some of them aren't telling the truth. Take the liars away and the ones that are left will spell out the peasant's nickname.

48

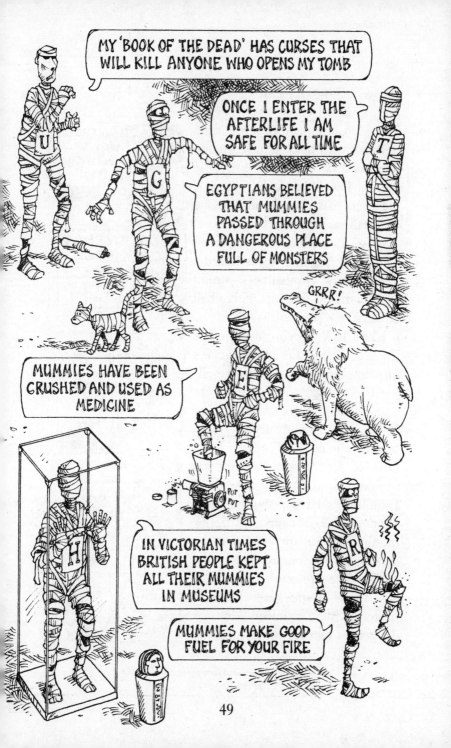

49

Answer: G-I-N-G-E-R
Here's why…

Y – No. Sometimes eyes were replaced with black stones, though Ramesses IV was given two little onions! They'd be pickled onions if they were soaked in natron. Imagine eating those with your chips.

G – Yes. Bits often fell off bodies – or maybe a passing jackal nicked a few fingers! Embalmers would replace the missing bits with a ball of linen or a piece of wood.

I – Yes. In Victorian times people flocked to Dr Pettigrew's unwrappings. They were a sell-out like today's pop concerts. On one occasion the Archbishop of Canterbury was turned away because the hall was full.

O – No. Dr Pettigrew's work was so popular that the Duke of Hamilton asked to be mummified – after his death, of course. Pettigrew mummified him in 1852 and the daft duke was buried in a stone coffin – like a pharaoh.

N – Yes. The spells were there to protect the mummy in its dangerous journey to the afterlife.

U – No. The 'Books of the Dead' were prayers of protection against evil spirits NOT curses. The 'Mummy's Curse' idea is nineteenth-century nonsense and twentieth-century tosh!

T – No. Once a person reaches the afterlife his heart will be weighed on a set of scales. If the heart is heavy with wickedness then he will be eaten by 'the Devourer' – a monster that is part crocodile, part hippopotamus and part lion.

G – Yes. Mummies, the Egyptians said, had boiling lakes and rivers of fire to cross before they reached the afterlife. There was also a snake that spat poison at them. The mummies needed their 'Book of the Dead' as a magic charm to ward off evil.

E – Yes. A thousand years after they were buried, some mummies were dug up and used as magical healing potions. A mummy could be ground into a powder. King Charles II of England sprinkled powdered mummy over himself to get some mummy greatness! Yeuch!

H – No. The Victorians bought and sold bits of mummy to decorate their houses! A mummy foot or hand in a glass case was quite common.

R – Yes. Dug-up mummies became so common 200 years ago that they were thrown into ovens. In the famous pharaohs' graveyard known as the Valley of the Kings (by the Nile), mummies were used as fuel so the poor people could eat.

You should end up with the word 'Ginger' – the mummy's nickname. The museum keepers called him that because he had red-brown hair.

But ... there is a story that 'Ginger' wasn't an Ancient Egyptian mummy after all. The British Museum collectors were tricked. They went to Egypt looking for mummies and a crooked dealer sold the Brits a fairly new corpse that he'd dried out!

There is even a story that the dealer sold them the corpse of his own brother!

Super sacrifices

The Egyptians believed everyone was made up of two parts – the body and the spirit. They called the spirit 'Ka'.

Your body might die but your Ka could live on ... if it had somewhere to live.

The best place for the Ka to live after death was in the person's dead body – and that's why bodies were mummified.

Even after death, the Ka could get hungry so people were buried with food and drink.

The gods worshipped by the Egyptians were Kas, and they lived in statues. But, just like humans, Ka corpses had to be fed. A mummy had to have its mouth opened so it could eat.

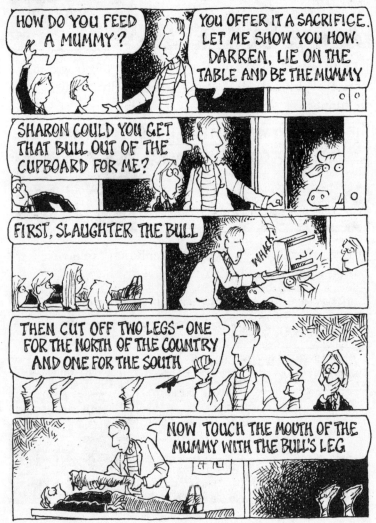

A SPECIAL TOOL WAS USED TO OPEN THE MUMMY'S MOUTH AND A PRAYER WAS READ. HERE'S A COPY. READ IT, TRACEY

THE MOUTH WAS CLOSED BUT I HAVE OPENED YOUR MOUTH AND TEETH, YOUR EYES WERE CLOSED BUT I HAVE OPENED THEM. I HAVE OPENED YOUR MOUTH WITH THE IRON TOOL THAT ANUBIS USED. THE DEAD WILL WALK AND TALK. HIS BODY WILL JOIN THE GODS IN THEIR HOUSE. HE SHALL BE GIVEN A CROWN BY HORUS

THEY FINISHED OFF BY SAYING, "YOU ARE YOUNG AGAIN, YOU SHALL LIVE AGAIN FOREVER"

...WISH HE'D TRY THAT ON ME

Mad mummies quiz

Don't wrap your mummy till you've tried this quick quiz. See how much you know before you begin binding with bandages. Score 10 and you are bound to be good.

1 The Arabs were the first to uncover ancient mummies. They thought the bodies were wrapped in something they called 'mumiya' – a sticky black stuff that goes hard. What would we call this stuff?
a) Bandages b) Tar
c) Toffee

2 When was the famous mummy of Tutankhamun dug up?
a) 1822 b) 1872 c) 1922

3 Some time between 1352 and 1336 BC King Akhenaten argued with his daughter and sent her for execution. What spiteful thing did he have done to the corpse?
a) Cut off its hair so no one would admire her beauty any more.
b) Cut off a hand so she couldn't go into the afterlife.
c) Cut off its finger to get a ring back.

4 What was the punishment for grave-robbing in Ancient Egypt?
a) Horrible torture
b) Horrible execution
c) Horrible torture followed by horrible execution

5 A grave robber reached into a coffin to steal some gold. The lid of the coffin fell and trapped him, then the roof of the tomb collapsed and killed him. He was found later, his skeleton hand still trapped in the coffin. How many years was his corpse there?

a) 26 years b) 260 years c) 2,600 years

6 A pharaoh's mother could be given a rich burial, too. The mother of Cheops had a burial shaft dug so deep that no one could rob her coffin. Yet they did. How?

a) They dug a tunnel through the rock to reach the coffin.
b) They hijacked the coffin on its way to the burial shaft.
c) They pinched the valuables before she was buried.

7 An 1880s tomb robber, Mohammed, was caught after selling the tomb treasures of 30 mummies. What did the Egyptians do with Mohammed?

a) They gave him a reward for finding the mummies.
b) They cut off his hands.
c) They cut off his head.

8 Archaeologists learn a lot from mummies. What do they learn from mummy teeth?

a) The ancient Egyptians used toothpaste.
b) The ancient Egyptians ate beef burgers.
c) Egyptian bread was coarse and gritty.

Answers:

1b) 'Mumiya' was the Arab word for tar. Of course the Arabs were wrong – it wasn't tar – but the name 'mumiya' has stuck ... like tar!

2c) It was found by the archaeologist Howard Carter in a burial chamber (not a pyramid). Carter was sponsored by Lord Carnarvon and Carnarvon died six months later – and that started the rumour of the mummy's curse!

3b) Only a complete body could pass into the afterlife so the cruel king was trying to prevent her enjoying Egyptian heaven! There is a story that the mummified hand was taken to England in the 1920s – and the girl's ghost haunted its owners.

4c) But this didn't stop the robbers. Their favourite trick was to bribe the tomb-makers and the guards to make the robbery easier. Sometimes the pharaoh's own priests helped in the robbery.

5a) The robber was trapped in the tomb and his greedy skeleton was found by archaeologists in 1970. They knew when he had died because in the skeleton's tattered coat was a newspaper – dated 1944.

6c) Modern archaeologists dug up the coffin of Cheops' mother, Hetepheres. It had not been disturbed, yet there were just two poor silver bracelets with the skeleton. Where was the fabulous treasure Cheops said he'd buried with her? It was nicked before the coffin was sealed. Khufu's prime minister, Yussef, is the chief suspect.

7a) Mohammed was rewarded for finding the mummies – which he hadn't touched. The Egyptian government 'forgot' about the loot he'd stolen and gave him a job … as a guide, showing tourists round the tombs.

8c) The teeth are usually badly worn down from eating bread. The corn was ground between stones and grit from the stones got into the flour. Eating bread must have been like eating sandpaper. Yeuch!

Did you know…?
Pharaohs were buried with mummies of animals. Cats were popular but they also made mummies out of …

The truth about Tutankhamun

King Tutankhamun was dead as a duck's toenail and he was buried in a rock tomb.

Did he rest in peace?

Not for long. If the Ancient Egyptians had had ancient policemen then the report might have looked like this:

 VALLEY OF THE KINGS CONSTABULARY

Crime: Grave robbing	**Date:** 1327 BC

Address: King Tutankhamun's Tomb,
Valley of the Kings, Egypt

Report: I was called to the tomb of King T. at 6 a.m. As I was asleep at the time I was not amused, I can tell you. 'Another kid been eaten by a croc?' I groaned.

'No, sir,' Sergeant Paneb said. 'King Tutankhamun's grave's been robbed.'

I sighed and turned over on the straw. 'That was yesterday, Sergeant,' I said. 'I looked into it. I looked into the case and I looked into the grave. The robbers had stolen bronze arrow-heads off the king's arrows, some fine materials and some perfume jars.'

'But sir,' Paneb tried to interrupt. He's always doing that.

'They were clever,' I told him. 'They only took things that could not be traced back to the tomb – I mean one arrow-head is pretty much like any other arrow-head ... unless it's in YOUR head, of course. They can do a bit of damage those arrow-heads.'

'But, sir –' he cut in. Did I mention he's always doing that?

'They tried to steal some golden furniture,' I went on. 'They thought they could melt it down. Then they found it was just wooden furniture covered in gold leaf. Hah! Threw it back in the tomb, didn't they?'

'But sir!' Paneb cried.

I shouted him down. 'The grave was sealed with tons of limestone chips. Grave closed, case closed,' I said and turned over to get some sleep.

'But, sir,' Paneb went on. 'They've robbed it again!'

'What? What?' I said and jumped off my straw bed. 'Why didn't you say so, you buffoon?'

'The robbers made a tunnel through the chippings and broke in again.'

'A tunnel? That must have taken them all night,' I said, looking for my tunic and sandals.

'Seven hours at least,' Paneb said. 'This time they got jewels out.'

'No clues?' I asked as I stumbled out into the morning air.

'Just this, sir,' Paneb said. He jangled a twisted scarf in front of me. When I opened it I found eight gold rings. 'I think they were in such a hurry to get away they dropped part of the loot.'

Eight rings – not much of a clue.

By the time I got to the grave the dead king's minister, Maya, was there. His face was like a stone statue. He glared at me. 'You are too late,' he snarled.

'It's never too late to catch a thief,' I told him brightly.

'It is,' he snapped. 'My guards caught them running away. You have failed.' He took a step towards me and poked me in the shoulder. I hate that. 'I will make Sergeant Paneb my new chief of police.'

'I'm out of a job?' I cried.

'Oh, no,' Maya said viciously. 'You have a new job – you can be the royal executioner. You can start with the grave robbers we caught.'

I groaned. Because we all know what happens to grave robbers, don't we?

Well? Do we?

The tomb of Tutankhamun WAS robbed twice shortly after his funeral. And a scarf, twisted round eight precious rings, WAS found in the tunnel that the robbers used.

We don't know if the ring robbers were caught or if they escaped. But we're pretty sure what would have happened to them if they had been caught. And it wasn't very nice.

If you were a pharaoh and someone was caught grave-robbing, what punishment would you give them?
a) Have them buried alive in the grave they tried to rob.
b) Have them sacrificed in the temple of Baba, the cannibal god.
c) Have them placed on a pole with a sharp end.

Answer: c) This is called impaling. But the victims weren't stabbed with the sharp pole. They were lowered on to it slowly. Their weight pressed down on the point – the more they struggled the further it tore into them. It was a slow and painful death.

You wouldn't want that to happen to you. But you wouldn't want to be the executioner either ... would you?

DUNNO, COULD BE PAYBACK
FOR MAKING A MUMMY OF ME

The curse of Tutankhamun's tomb

Mummies are a bit creepy. Looking at corpses of long-dead people is enough to give you goosebumps on your goosebumps. But it's just not creepy enough for some people!

Some people like to imagine the mummies aren't just shrivelled flesh – they believe the mummy spirits wander around, putting curses on the living people who disturbed their rest and robbed their graves!

Tutankhamun's tomb was discovered in 1922 and started a wave of 'curse' rumours but *Horrible Histories* has found out the truth. Someone at some time has said all the following ten stories are true. Can you work out which stories are simple LIES (L), which are MISTAKES (M) and which are TRUE (T) but can be explained?

1 The Earl of Carnarvon paid for the expedition to dig up the mummy of Tutankhamun and he died within six months of the discovery. L or M or T?

2 When Tutankhamun's mummy was unwrapped the archaeologists found a curse wrapped in the bandages. It said: 'Those who enter this sacred tomb shall swiftly be visited by the wings of death.' L or M or T?

3 Lord Carnarvon's friend, Count Hamon, owned an ancient mummy's hand. It was as soft and fresh as the day it was cut off the mummy. L or M or T?

4 Lord Carnarvon pricked his cheek on a poisoned arrow–head in the tomb and died from the poison. L or M or T?

5 When Lord Carnarvon died his favourite dog howled at the exact moment of his death. The dog was 3,000 miles away in England. L or M or T?

6 Mohammed Ibrahim had been very much against moving Tutankhamun's treasures to France in 1966. He fought to keep the mummy in Egypt, but he lost the fight in a final meeting. Ibrahim left the meeting — and walked into the path of a taxi. He died instantly. L or M or T?

7 A worker in the British Museum was fastening labels to items stolen from Tutankhamun's tomb. He dropped dead. L or M or T?

8 Arthur Mace was one of the first people to enter the tomb and he died shortly afterwards. L or M or T?

9 American millionaire George Gould visited the tomb. He was fine before he went but died soon after. L or M or T?

10 The mummy's 'curse' is in fact Ancient Egyptian germs that were sealed into the tomb 3,000 years ago. L or M or T?

Answers:

1 **True, but** … Carnarvon was a sickly man. He'd been in a car accident a while before the mummy-discovery and was not fit for the heat of Egypt.

2 **Lies.** A newspaper reported this curse soon after Carnarvon's death. The mummies were buried with a 'Book of the Dead' in their coffins. Some people believe this book cursed grave robbers. The truth is that the 'Book of the Dead' was a collection of prayers and charms to protect the person's spirit in the next life. It was not a curse book.

3 **Lies.** Hamon did indeed own a mummy hand, but he made a lot of money as a fortune-teller. It suited him to tell stories about ghostly experiences.

4 **Mistake.** Lord Carnarvon got a mosquito bite on his face – not a poison-arrow scratch. He cut it open when he was shaving and that gave him blood poisoning and a fever. He was very weak and caught a lung infection. That's what killed him, not the scratch on the face.

5 **True, but** … this was just a creepy story told by Lord Carnarvon's son. But what has it to do with a mummy's curse? Another story said all the lights in Egypt's capital city Cairo went out at that moment. Again, creepy – but nothing to do with the 'curse'?

6 **True, but** … this was a 'friend' of the mummy trying to keep it in Egypt. Surely the curse wouldn't have affected him?

7 **Lies.** The British Museum never had any objects from Tut's tomb.

8 **True, but** … Mace had been ill before he entered the tomb. He had pleurisy and there was no cure for this illness in 1922.

9 **Mistake.** Gould was not in good health before his visit. He went to Egypt because he was ill and thought the warm weather would help. He did visit the tomb, but the stress of the travelling killed him.

10 **Mistake.** The air in the tomb wouldn't be very healthy, but King Tut's germs wouldn't kill a visitor today.

Did you know…?
In March 1923, a writer named Marie Corelli (real name Mary Mackay) wrote the following warning…

There will be terrible danger for anyone who enters the tomb of Tutankhamun!

What made mad Marie say that? Well, on the day Howard Carter opened the tomb, his pet canary was swallowed by a cobra, and cobras were the guards of the pharaohs!

Poor tweeter. But the canary hadn't gone into the tomb – Carter had. What happened to him?

a) He was swallowed by a cobra the next day.
b) He swallowed a cobra and lived another two days.
c) He lived another 17 years, dying just before his sixty-fifth birthday.

Answer: c) Not much of a curse!

Scotch missed bone

Don't go to No. 15 Learmonth Gardens in Edinburgh!

Oh, very well. Go there if you must. But beware the mummy's curse … I said, the mummy's curse.[7]

In 1936 Sir Alexander Hay Seton went to Egypt. He and his wife Zeyla visited a tomb. A guide led them down a stone staircase into an underground room.

'These are the bones of an ancient princess,' the guide said, and he showed A and Z a crumbling mummy.

When no one was looking Zeyla slipped a bit of bone from the mummy into her handbag. Was she potty about a patella or crazy for a cranium? No, she was batty for a bit of backbone.

She took it home to 15 Learmonth Gardens in Edinburgh and put it in a glass case[8]. Then the trouble started.

As Sir Alex left the house one day a piece of the roof crashed down and missed him by a whisker.

Furniture was broken. A table turned over in the night.

Sounds disturbed the sleep of the horrified Hay Setons.

Ornaments rose in the air and flew across the room.

7 There should be at lease ten exclamation marks here to add a bit of drama! I can't be bothered to type ten exclamation marks so I'll leave a space and you can add your own.

8 It is always best to put your stolen bones in a glass case. Especially if they are leg bones. The case stops them from running away. But this was a spine bone – a glass case was clearly a mistake because the bone was spyin' on them.

Worst of all, the ghostly figure of an Egyptian priest popped up from time to time. Visitors and servants all saw it.

A newspaper reporter heard about the curse and asked if he could borrow the bone.

Sir Alex sent the bone on loan (alone). The reporter came back two weeks later. 'Nothing happened,' he laughed. But a few days later he was desperately ill in hospital.

Sir Alex lost his money when business went wrong.

'It's the curse of the stolen bone!' Sir Alex moaned. 'Destroy it!' he ordered.

Zeyla would not hear of it.

Sir Alex was too lazy to destroy it himself (you could say he was bone idle) so he went to his cousin who was a monk. First the monk blessed it, then he destroyed it. The bone was burned to ashes in a stove.

Zeyla could not forgive Alex, so she left him.

Alex wrote...

> *The curse did not end with the bone being burned. From 1936 onwards trouble seemed to follow me wherever I went.*

He died in 1963 at the age of 58.

Misery for Menkaure

Pharaohs didn't just leave curses behind. Sometimes the pharaoh himself was cursed.

The gods told Menkaure that he would die in six years' time.

He decided to cheat the gods. Menkaure gave orders for candles to be burned after dark so, in his palace, there was never any day or night. The Pharaoh lived day AND night, so he said he lived twelve years – not six.

Then he died.

But WHY was he cursed?

a) He was too cruel to the peasants.

b) He was too kind to the peasants.

c) He was too cruel to his granny.

Answer: b) Menkaure was not as harsh as the other pharaohs. That upset the gods who said he SHOULD have been. Bet the peasants were pleased.

Cruel crime time

Ancient Egypt was as full of crime as the Wild West in the USA or the dark streets of Victorian London.

And the crimes haven't changed much since the days of the pharaohs – murder, theft and cruelty. Times change – people don't.

Here are a few horribly historical crime stories from Ancient Egypt...

PLAN TO BAM RAM!

1151 BC – There was a plot to murder Ramesses III, hatched by one of his wives, Tiy. The plan was to attack Ramesses inside his palace while rebels started a revolt in the cities outside.

The plotters were caught and their sentence would have been death. But unusually the judges said...

YOU MUST TAKE YOUR OWN LIFE AND YOU MUST DO IT NOW, HERE IN THIS COURT

That must have made a right mess on the court floor.

LAW AND DISORDER

What do you do with a judge who breaks the law?

In the Ramesses trial a couple of the judges were caught having dinner with the plotters. It was their turn to be put on trial. The judges' judge said...

I SENTENCE YOU TO HAVE YOUR NOSE AND EARS SLICED OFF

One of the crooked judges killed himself before the executioner could carve him. The other had a bit of Egyptian plastic surgery...

I'LL NEVER HEAR ANOTHER CASE AGAIN

FAILED NILE MEANS NASTY NIBBLES

The Nile flooded every year and watered the crops. The farmers gathered the corn and it lasted them a year till the next flood.

But when the Nile failed to flood there was no food. What did they do?

Around 1900 BC there was a famine. The Egyptian Heqanakhte left his family in Thebes to go in search of food in the north. He wrote a letter home that told a foul famine tale…

I HAVE ARRIVED HERE AMD AM COLLECTING AS MUCH FOOD AS POSSIBLE. IT IS NOT MUCH AS THE NILE IS LOW HERE TOO. NO ONE WANTS TO SELL FOOD. THEY HAVE STARTED TO EAT PEOPLE HERE. TRY TO HOLD OUT TILL I RETURN

Heqanakhte doesn't say if they were eating corpses or killing people. (Corpses can be old and chewy – much better to kill a nice fresh feller.)

GIVEN A GOOD HIDE-ING

In 1315 BC the Pharaoh Ay died … aye, die he did. Horemheb, an army general, seized power and passed laws to look after the poor.

He was worried that too many soldiers were stealing cattle-skins (hides) from the lower classes. So he made a new punishment for hide thieves…

STICK UP FOR THIEVES

Seti I had his laws carved into a cliff at Nauri. The gods in the temple owned cattle in the area. If you stole cattle from a god you had a really nasty punishment waiting for you – impaling.

Seti's law said…

PUNISHMENT FOR A CATTLE THIEF WILL BE CASTING HIM DOWN AND IMPALING HIM ON A STAKE. HIS WIFE AND CHILDREN WILL BECOME SLAVES

That means a sharp pole was placed into the ground. The thief was taken to a cliff and thrown down on to the point.

A sharp lesson.

Ruthless robbers

Great Egyptians were buried with great wealth. Poor Egyptians wanted it, so they robbed the graves. They stole the gold to melt it and sell it. They didn't mind what damage they did.

Of course all the graves have been robbed by now – some were robbed at the time of the burial and many were cleaned out by greedy treasure hunters in the nineteenth century.

The robbers said:

WE ARE COLLECTING HISTORICAL MATERIAL FOR YOUR EDUCATION

That's a bit like a bank robber saying…

MY HOBBY IS COLLECTING BANK NOTES

… they're all just robbers!

In 1901 a British historian, Flinders[9] Petrie, was 'exploring' Pharaoh Dojer's tomb. He found an arm wrapped in bandages stuffed into a crack in the wall. No one is sure how it got there.

Maybe an early robber had ripped it off and hidden it. Other grave robbers had not seen the arm – or the rich bracelets on the wrist.

One pharaoh went to amazing lengths to keep robbers away from his grave…

9 Cinders may be short for Cinderella. But Flinders is not short for Flinderella – just thought you'd like to know.

A-Maze-ing Amenemhet

Pharaoh Amenemhet was worried about his funeral…

But Amenemhet was worried about robbers stealing his body after it was buried. You don't have any fear of that, do you?

Amenemhet needed a plan to keep thieves away from his tomb. He believed that his burial room had to be filled with riches if he was to be comfortable in the afterlife. But he had learned his lesson from other dead pharaohs, who had ordered that the passages of their pyramids be plugged with massive granite blocks after the burial. Tomb robbers had simply cut through the softer limestone walls around them. They found the burial rooms and grabbed the treasures.

How could Amenemhet stop them?

Sadly machine guns hadn't been invented. No – he needed something so clever that no one would ever find their way in to the centre of the tomb.

He decided to build a pyramid where the passages inside were a maze. There would be secret sliding doors, false corridors, and hidden rooms.

No one but the Pharaoh himself knew all the secrets. The workmen who built the maze were led to their work each day with blindfolds on.

Since Amenemhet was the only one who knew the way through his amazing tomb, we should get him to tell us the route...

ONCE A THIEF HAS CARVED THROUGH THESE BLOCKS, HE WILL DISCOVER HE HAS BEEN TRICKED – THE PASSAGEWAY IS A DEAD END

THE RIGHT PATH IS A CORRIDOR CLOSED ONLY BY A WOODEN DOOR

THIS OPENS INTO ANOTHER DEAD-END PASSAGE

TO GET OUT OF THIS PASSAGE YOU HAVE TO FIND A HIDDEN SLIDING STONE

YOU FIND YOURSELF IN A BARE ROOM; FROM HERE A SECRET TRAPDOOR LEADS TO A LONG PASSAGEWAY FILLED IN WITH MASSIVE STONE BLOCKS

BREAK THROUGH THE BLOCKS AND FIND TWO OPEN BURIAL SHAFTS IN THE FLOOR. ONE IS FILLED IN BY STONE SLABS; THE OTHERS SEEM TO BE EMPTY

Now, the question is, did it work?
Was Amenemhet's tomb...
a) robbed in ancient times?
b) safe until the twentieth century?

Answer: a) Somehow, tomb robbers got through all these defences. They emptied the burial chamber but, angry at all the dead ends, they took a horrible revenge. They set fire to Amenemhet's mummy, ensuring that he would not live in the afterlife.

It seems as though grave robbers would stop at nothing to steal a pharaoh's treasures.

Loret's horror

In 1898 a French historian named Victor Loret explored the tomb of Amenhotep II. He hoped to find a coffin and a neatly wrapped mummy. Instead he found something out of a horror movie.

He described it in his diary…

- I had only a candle for light and almost stumbled into a well - a deep pit used to catch the water when the Valley of the Kings flooded.

- I placed a ladder over the ugly hole and crawled over to the other side. I was in a small room. Broken statues were scattered over the floor.

- Thieves had been there before me. A doorway led into another room. That was where I hoped to find the mummy.

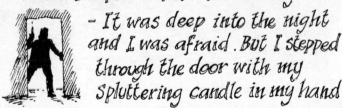

- It was deep into the night and I was afraid. But I stepped through the door with my spluttering candle in my hand

- A horrible sight met my eyes. There was a small boat in the room - the boat built to carry the Pharaoh to the next world.

- But in place of the mummy there was a corpse, black and grinning. Its face was turned towards me. I felt it was staring at me.

- Its long, brown hair was in clumps around its head. I never dreamed I was looking at a mummy that had been torn from its wrapping.

- There was a hole in its chest and another in its skull. I thought I was looking at the victim of a human sacrifice

- Or was this a tomb robber who had been killed by the other robbers and left to rot alone down here?

- Was it, maybe, a thief who had been caught by the guards and killed on the spot? And still the eyes stared at me!

Loret had found the mummy of a prince. It had been unwrapped soon after it had been buried – the thieves had been looking for jewels wrapped in its bandages.

Loret's shocks were not over, though. He found three other exposed mummies in the other rooms – a man, a woman and a boy.

The male mummy was King Amenhotep II. Some of the padding had been torn from its mouth in the search for jewels. A strip of cloth hung out like a dead tongue.

There were nine more coffins in the tomb. These contained nine wrecked mummies, which had been collected by King Pinedjem I in ancient times.

But thieves had got at them a second time.

Would YOU unwrap a corpse and smash open its body to steal its jewels?

Did you know …?

You shouldn't feel too sorry for Amenhotep II. When he was alive he was pretty ruthless. In his 1425 BC battles against the Nubians he captured seven enemy princes and wanted them killed as sacrifices to the gods. Normally that job would have been given to an executioner. Amenhotep II killed them himself.

SACRIFICING? OOOOH! COULD I...YOU KNOW...IF IT'S OK WITH YOU THAT IS...HAVE A GO?

Rotten religion

The Egyptians told many stories about their gods. The trouble with Egyptian gods is that they all got a bit mixed up. Their stories were repeated for 3,000 years and they changed over time.

The sun god, Re, became mixed up with Amun (the god of the city of Thebes) and by around 1500 BC he had become one god – Amun-Re.

And the moon god Thoth sometimes appears as an ibis bird and sometimes as a baboon!

Great gods

There were two sorts of gods in Egypt – the great gods that looked after the whole country … and the little gods that looked after your house and family.

The great gods had temples and were fed with fat, fleshy sacrifices. The little gods didn't get so much as a stale bag of crisps. (Probably because crisps hadn't been invented.)

Here are some of the groovy gods you could have prayed to in Ancient Egypt.

1. AMUN (sometimes called Amoun or Amun-Ra)
Looks like … an ape, or a man with the head of a frog.
Worship him because … he's the top man, 'the king of the gods'.

HIS NICKNAME WAS THE GREAT HONKER BECAUSE HE HONKED LIKE A GOOSE

2. ANUBIS

Looks like … a man with the head of a jackal (or a dog).
Worship him because … he's the main mummy man.

HE WRAPPED UP BITS OF THE DEAD OSIRIS AND BROUGHT HIM BACK TO LIFE – A USEFUL TRICK – ANUBIS IS A GOOD GOD TO KNOW

3. HATHOR

Looks like … a woman with the ears of a cow, or a cow or a woman with horns and a sun disc on her head.
Worship her because … she's the goddess of music, dance and booze.

SHE IS A USEFUL GODDESS FOR KEEPING YOUR GRASS SHORT. COW… GRAZING… GEDDIT? OH NEVER MIND YOU PROBABLY DON'T WANT A DANCING COW ON YOUR LAWN ANYWAY

4. HORUS

Looks like … a hawk or a man with the head of a falcon.
Worship him because … he looks after children and the pharaoh – and he can cure snake bites.

HE'S UP THERE IN THE SKY LOOKING AFTER YOUR PHARAOH

5. ISIS

Looks … similar to Hathor. Often shown with horns and sun disc.

Worship her because …
she's Horus's Mum.

> HER WINGS BREATHE LIFE INTO THE DEAD

6. KHEPRI

Looks like … a scarab or dung beetle.

Worship him because … he's the new-born sun god. He rolls the sun across the sky each day like a dung beetle rolls a ball of poo.

> DUNG BEETLES OFTEN POP OUT OF THE POO THEY'VE BEEN SLEEPING IN. THE EGYPTIANS THOUGHT THEY HAD HATCHED OUT OF NOTHING, SO KHEPRI WAS A GOD WHO CREATED HIMSELF

7. KHNUM

Looks like … a man with the head of a ram.

Worship him because … he's the god of the Nile and the pots that are made from its mud. He made people on his potter's wheel.

> WE'RE ALL HERE THANKS TO THIS MUDDY, MODELLING GOD

8. OSIRIS

Looks like … a man chopped into pieces then joined together again and wrapped in white linen like a mummy. His skin is green. He carries a shepherd's crook and a flail to make corn into flour.

Worship him because … he's another top god.

> HE WILL LOOK AFTER YOU WHEN YOU DIE

9. SETH

Looks like … a man with the head of a strange beast. Enough to give you nightmares.

Worship him because … he's the nasty brother of Osiris and son of Nut.[10] God of trouble.

> HE CHOPPED OSIRIS UP INTO BITS

10. THOTH

Looks like … one of three shapes – a baboon or an ibis bird or a man with an ibis's head. (Never as a man with a baboon's head. If you see one of those it's probably a history teacher.)

Worship him because … he's the god of writing and wisdom.

> WORSHIP HIM BECAUSE THEN YOU WILL DO WELL IN SCHOOL AND WHEN YOU DIE HE'S THE GOD WHO RECORDS THE WEIGHT OF YOUR HEART. A GOOD HEART WILL GET YOU INTO HEAVEN

10 No, no, no! Not the son of a nut. The son of Nut – goddess of the sky. Maybe she should have given savage Seth a crack round the ear when he was a kid. A sort of Nut cracker.

Horus horror

The god Horus had two eyes. Nothing new there then. But along came savage Uncle Seth and ripped out his left eye. He then tore the eye to pieces.

Horus FOUND the pieces of his left eye and popped them back in. But it was never as strong as his right eye.

Horus let his eyes float over the Earth to light it. The sun is the strong right eye, the Moon is his weak left eye.

Temple brain-teaser

Enter the Temple of Mystery. Can you match the right god to the gruesome stories?

If you can then *Horrible Histories* will award you a special prize –

WIN A TRIP -TO- EGYPT

FOR ONE LUCKY READER AND THEIR FAMILY
SIMPLY ANSWER TEN *EASY* QUESTIONS
SEND YOUR ENTRY WITH A £100 NOTE TO:
'*The Great Terry Deary Egypt Scam, Cairo*'

Small print. Please note, this offer applies only to readers over the age of 90 who are dead and mummified. Normal terms and conditions apply.

Even smaller print. Winners must be accompanied on the trip by their parents and pay for their own travel, meals and accommodation.

The middle column will give you a clue — as if an awesome Egyptian expert like you needs them!

Name	Clue	Story

1. Ammit — lion front and hippo bum

Munch!

A. Murders humans and feasts on their guts

2. Duamutef — head of jackal, body of man

Gutsy!

B. Looks after lungs of mummy

3. Hapy — baboon head, body of man

Chesty!

C. Sneezed and his snot became the gods

4. Nut — a cow

Gulp!

D. Known as 'She who Loves Silence'

5. Mafdet — a panther

Ssss!

E. Was a dung beetle that rolled its eggs into a ball of animal

6. Meretseger – cobra shape

Shhh!

F. Looks after intestines of mummy

7. Baba – baboon

Dangerous!

G. Guards you against snake bites

8. Atum – man with a crown

Atchoo!

H. Eats evil hearts on judgement day

9. Sekhmet – a lioness

Guzzle!

I. Started to massacre all humans until she got too drunk

10. Khepri – god of the sun

Pooh!

J. Swallows the sun every night

Did you know…?

A peasant like you could become a god/dess. Gods were usually dead kings, but ordinary people could become gods too if they died in a certain way. How did they have to die?

a) By falling off a pyramid

b) Dying in battle saving a pharaoh

c) By drowning in the Nile

Answer: c) The River Nile was the most important thing in Egypt. Without its flooding there would just be a desert and no great nation. So the river became holy. And from around 1550 BC anyone who drowned in the River Nile could become a god and have their own little temple! So, you want to become an Egyptian god? Go take a long walk off a short plank over the Nile!

Killing ... and curing

It can be horrible if you are ill. But sometimes the cure is worse than the illness.

Which would you rather have? The pain of toothache ... or the pain of a drill whizzing round your mouth?

But you are lucky. Lucky you weren't an Egyptian. If you had a broken bone then the doctor would mix a paste and slap it on...

I MIX THE BERRIES OF CORIANDER, POPPY PLANT, JUNIPER AND SAMES PLANT WITH SOME HONEY

I PUT THE MIXTURE ON A BANDAGE AND I WRAP THE BANDAGE ROUND THE BROKEN BONE

E!

FINALLY I DRAW ON THE MAGIC EYE OF HORUS, THE FALCON GOD

NOW DRINK THIS WINE WITH CRUSHED EGGSHELL IN IT TO HELP YOU HEAL

The cure for a broken nose was to…

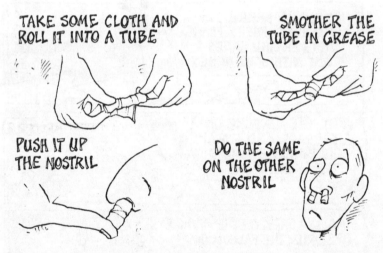

TAKE SOME CLOTH AND ROLL IT INTO A TUBE

SMOTHER THE TUBE IN GREASE

PUSH IT UP THE NOSTRIL

DO THE SAME ON THE OTHER NOSTRIL

Nice.

But these weren't the only disgusting cures.

Is your teacher going bald? Then offer him a mixture of viper's oil mixed with bats' ears[11]. Crush them all together and slap them on the bald patch.

The Egyptian cure for toothache is so disgusting I can't even tell you what it was!

What? You REALLY want to know? Oh, very well…

11 Or maybe not. Bats are protected species … and I haven't a clue what 'viper's oil' is.

Horrible Histories warning:
Do NOT read this if you are under the age of 75, suffer from nightmares, or faint at the thought of blood.

The cure was written down by the Greek visitor to Egypt, Hippocrates. But he was a bit odd. He thought you could make toothpaste by crushing three mice in the head of a hare.

One book for Egyptian doctors describes how to deal with a nasty cut...

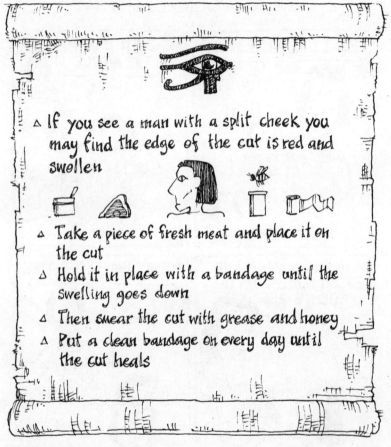

△ If you see a man with a split cheek you may find the edge of the cut is red and swollen

△ Take a piece of fresh meat and place it on the cut

△ Hold it in place with a bandage until the swelling goes down

△ Then smear the cut with grease and honey

△ Put a clean bandage on every day until the cut heals

Did you know...?

The Egyptians were sure that all illness was a result of what you ate. So they liked to diet and take herbs that would make all the poo run out of them for three days – sort of a clear-out. The servant who looked after the pharaoh's 'clear out' was known as the 'Shepherd of the Royal Backside'.

The 'Doctor! Doctor!' quiz

Could you become an Egyptian doctor? Here's a test to see if you're a medical mastermind…

The Egyptian doctors treated people with a mixture of medicine and magic. Some may have cured but others probably killed. Look at some of the Egyptian beliefs about death and doctoring and make up your own mind.

1 In England in the 1920s people were still using an Ancient Egyptian cure for children who wet the bed. What did the child have to eat?

a) A cooked mouse
b) A cooked louse
c) A crooked house

2 The Egyptians had a cure for night-blindness that modern doctors think may have worked. What did the Egyptians drink?

a) Blood from a white cat's tail
b) Juice from an ox's liver
c) Pee from a greyhound

3 The Egyptians used clever cures like onion juice (an antibiotic) and some horrible ones. In some medical scrolls the Egyptians describe how to make medicine using 19 different types of what?

a) Pee
b) Poo
c) Plum

97

4 The Egyptian cure for a burn was to cover it in a stuff that really worked. What?
a) Jam b) Honey c) Money

Answers:

1a) In Egypt the bones of the mouse were NOT eaten but wrapped in a cloth and the cloth hung round the neck of the child.

2b) Animal liver is high in vitamin A and could help some types of night-blindness.

3b) Medicines were made from all sorts of poo – from fly droppings to ostrich poo.

4b) Honey was put on the wound and probably worked in a lot of cases. It is an antibiotic (so the Egyptians made a lucky guess), but they believed that evil spirits hated honey and would be driven off by it. (Not such a good guess.)

Woeful workers

Have parents and teachers ever told you to work hard at school? What do they say?

Some schools used to say...

WORK HARD OR I'LL BEAT YOU!

Parents may threaten...

WORK HARD OR I'LL STOP YOUR POCKET MONEY

But the oldest threat is...

WORK HARD OR YOU'LL END UP WITH A TERRIBLE JOB

LIKE TEACHING

In fact this threat is so old that the Ancient Egyptians used it to bully their children. A man called Dua-Khety wrote down these threats for his son Pepi around 2000 BC. He makes life in Egypt sound horrible. Here is the top ten of terrible tradesmen...

SEE THE COPPER-WORKER SLAVING AT THE FURNACE, HIS FINGERS ARE LIKE CROCODILE CLAWS AND HE STINKS LIKE FISH POO[12]

THE REED-CUTTER GOES TO THE RIVER WHERE GNATS STING HIM AND SAND-FLEAS BITE HIM

THE POTTER IS COVERED IN EARTH TILL HIS CLOTHES ARE STIFF WITH MUD AND HIS HEAD CLOTH IS A RAG

THE BRICK-MAKER IS WORN OUT WITH SQUEEZING THE ANIMAL DROPPINGS TO MAKE BRICKS-AND HE EATS HIS BREAD WITHOUT WASHING HIS HANDS

THE FARM-WORKER HAS FINGERS COVERED IN SORES THAT TURN BAD AND SMELL ROTTEN

THE WEAVER SPENDS ALL DAY WITH HIS KNEES DRAWN UP TO HIS BELLY, IF HE LOSES A DAY'S WORK HE IS GIVEN 50 LASHES

12 This is an odd thing to say. How does the father know what fish poo smells like? Do YOU know what fish poo smells like? Where would you get the fish poo to find out? Where would you find a fish toilet?

THE MESSENGER FACES DANGERS ON THE ROAD — HE MIGHT BE TORN APART BY LIONS OR BEATEN BY ROBBERS

THE FURNACE-WORKER HAS SORE RED EYES AND HANDS THAT SMELL LIKE A CORPSE

THE WASHER-MAN WORKS AT THE RIVER AND IS IN DANGER FROM CROCODILES. HE EATS FOOD THAT IS MIXED WITH FILTH

THE FISHERMAN FALLS IN THE RIVER, WHERE HE MAY BE CRUSHED IN THE JAWS OF A HIPPO

So you see, the message is…

WORK HARD AT SCHOOL OR YOU MAY END UP WITH A TERRIBLE JOB

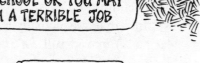

LIKE TEACHING

Did you know…?

Some history books say that the Ancient Egyptians had camels to do all their work. In 2000 BC the pharaoh gave camels to Abraham as a gift.

YES! IT SAYS SO IN THE BIBLE – GENESIS, CHAPTER 12, VERSE 16

The *Horrible Histories* truth is… they didn't. No one tamed a camel till around 1000 BC.

Super Scribes

The best job in Ancient Egypt was being a scribe – their job was to write. The scribe was his own boss, made lots of money and paid no taxes! What a life!

Trainee scribes spent seven years in scribe school, copying teacher's writing the way you copy off a whiteboard.

These young scribes would…

- Make their own pens by chewing the end of a reed to create a sort of paintbrush
- Carry a few different sizes of paintbrush-pens by sticking them behind their ears
- Use 'ink' that was actually a block of soot and gum (for black ink) or red soil for red ink. They would use the blocks of ink the way a modern painter uses watercolours.

So – got your reed? Chewed the end? Then you're ready to begin your training.

Here are a few foul Egyptian facts for you to copy – but first you have to fill in the missing words.

Missing words: statue, book, pig, severed hand, bag of corn, leopard, wooden beard, lettuce, woman, barrel of beer.

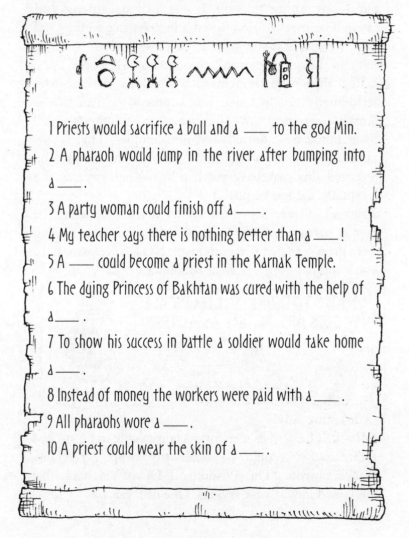

1 Priests would sacrifice a bull and a ___ to the god Min.

2 A pharaoh would jump in the river after bumping into a ___.

3 A party woman could finish off a ___.

4 My teacher says there is nothing better than a ___!

5 A ___ could become a priest in the Karnak Temple.

6 The dying Princess of Bakhtan was cured with the help of a ___.

7 To show his success in battle a soldier would take home a ___.

8 Instead of money the workers were paid with a ___.

9 All pharaohs wore a ___.

10 A priest could wear the skin of a ___.

Answers:

1 Lettuce. At the harvest festival the priests offered a holy bull some corn. If it ate the corn then that was a good sign – but not for the bull. It was then slaughtered and eaten! The priests also offered a holy lettuce to the God Min. Lettuce was supposed to be a love potion – so offer some to that girl/boy you fancy and see if it works!

2 Pig. Pigs were thought to be unclean. Anyone who accidentally touched one was supposed to run to the nearest river and throw him/herself in – clothes and all! Swineherds were not allowed into temples. That is sow unfair! (Some historians think the Ancient Greek who reported this may have got it a bit wrong, because the Egyptians ate lots of pork.)

3 Barrel of beer. Egyptian women drank as much as the men at parties. You had to drink your host's beer till you were drunk. In fact it was an insult NOT to get drunk. In one tomb painting a woman announces,

Charming lady!

4 Book. The scribes were important people in Egypt and their teachers could be really top people. Egyptian teachers wrote 'The Wisdom of Duauf', a book that contained lots of wise sayings. One of these was:

LEARN TO LOVE BOOKS – THERE IS NOTHING BETTER THAN BOOKS!

Three thousand years later teachers are STILL saying that! (Or it could simply be that your teachers are three thousand years old.)

5 Woman. Usually women were not allowed to be priests – a bit like the Christian church until the end of the twentieth century. But around 1000 BC one of the pharaoh's daughters became a priest.

6 Statue. The pharaoh's sister-in-law was ill and her family begged him to send a statue of the Egyptian moon god, Khonsu. He did and it worked. Remember that next time you pig out on too much chocolate cake and become ill: all you need is a statue!

7 Severed hand. Egyptian soldiers chopped off the right hands of dead enemies. This allowed the pharaohs to count the number of dead. Sometimes they cut off the enemies' naughty bits and Egyptian war paintings often show piles of these stacked up!

King Menephta of Egypt once took home the naughty bits of 1,300 Libyan soldiers killed in a battle that he won.

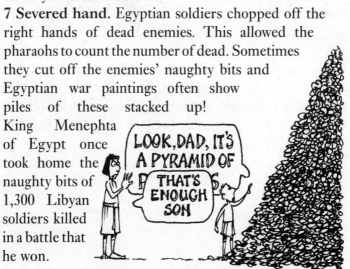

LOOK, DAD, IT'S A PYRAMID OF

THAT'S ENOUGH SON

8 Bag of corn. And in the reign of Ramesses III the workers didn't get their corn on time. They went on strike – the first strike in history. Corny but true.

9 Wooden beard. Of course the pharaoh was the number-one priest – and priests had no hair. The king showed he was really grown-up by having a beard. How do you have a beard if you have no hair? Wear a false one, made of wood or woven plant-fibre. It was hung on wires from a band around his forehead. When he died he swapped it for a godly beard – one that is plaited and turned up at the ends. Very fashionable in heaven, of course.

10 Leopard. Usually priests would wear no animal skin at all – no leather sandals or belts. But the skin of a leopard (or a cheetah) was worn by the chief priest. It was worn like a cloak with the head of the animal hanging over his right shoulder. Grr-reat idea.

Awful army

Egypt suffered a lot from invasions by bandits (who wanted to pinch their cattle). They suffered attacks from tribes like 'the Sea People', who had lost their own land, and from other nations, like the Hittites, who wanted the power and wealth of Egypt.

Being an Egyptian soldier could be hard work. In 1381 BC Amenhotep III's son crushed a revolt in Nubia. In just one hour the Egyptian soldiers captured and massacred 1,000 Nubians.

It was chop till you drop.

But a soldier's life may not have been as bad as Egyptian writers tried to make out. One Egyptian school book said...

The common soldier has many, many officers all telling him what to do. The officers say things like, "Get the men to work!" So the common soldier is woken after just an hour's sleep and worked until sunset. He is always hungry. He is a dead man yet he lives.

Around 1190 BC a teacher wrote...

A soldier is taken to an army camp while he is still a child. There he is given a beating. A wound is cut over his eyebrows. His head is split open with a wound. He is laid on the floor and trampled like reed-paper. When he goes to war he is loaded down like an ass till his back is breaking. He drinks foul water and gets to the battle like a plucked chicken.

Fighting fellers

How much do you know about the pharaoh's fighting fellers. Try this tricky test.

Which is the odd one out in these groups?

1 A soldier's weapons were: a stone-headed club, a spear, a bronze axe, a poison dart blower.

2 A common soldier protected himself with: a shield, a mop of thick hair, a helmet, a linen apron.

3 When the army wasn't at war the soldiers had other jobs: policemen, messengers, palace guards, firemen.

4 A soldier's chariot had: tyres, weapon-racks, doors, two horses.

5 An Egyptian army travelled with: laundry women, weapon-makers, cooks, writers.

Answers:

The odd ones out are:

1 A poison dart blower. The main weapon was the club (known today as a 'mace') to beat your enemy's brains out.

2 A helmet. Only the officers had helmets. The ordinary soldiers grew their hair thick to take the club blows and wore an apron to protect their naughty bits. Apart from that they didn't wear much – not even shoes.

3 Firemen. The Egyptians had a good messenger service and soldiers took news from fortress to fortress so the pharaoh always knew what was happening. These forts were about 80 kilometres apart. They also used soldiers as a police force and of course to parade as the pharaoh's guardsmen.

4 Doors. The Egyptians learned from Asia how to use horses, but never rode them in battle – they only used them to pull chariots. Their chariots usually carried a driver and a warrior. The floor was made of woven leather because a solid floor would have given a bouncy, travel-sick-making ride. The wheels had leather tyres to hold them together. (They didn't have strong glue and screws in those days!)

5 Laundry women. As the soldiers only wore an apron they didn't need anyone to do their washing for them. But they did take an army of cooks and weapon-makers and porters to carry their food and beer.

Dodgy Djehuty

Pharaoh Tuthmosis III made the Egyptians masters of the Middle East. But he did it with the help of generals like Djehuty.

Djehuty knew what all good generals know – if you can't win a battle fair and square, then cheat.

The town of Joppa rebelled and Djehuty realized that it would be nearly impossible to capture it by fighting fair. So this is what he did...

1 Djehuty went to Pharaoh Tuthmosis and said he could capture Joppa with just 200 men, 200 wine jars and 200 donkeys.

2 Djehuty went to Joppa and made a camp outside the city. He disguised himself as a messenger and took a letter to the Prince of Joppa. The message said that General Djehuty wanted to betray Egypt and join Joppa. It invited the Prince to meet the general in his camp.

110

3 Djehuty then went back to camp and dressed himself as the top Egyptian general (which he was). The Prince of Joppa arrived with his bodyguards and the two men chatted alone in a tent. The prince was desperate to know about the magic staff.

4 What happened next was that Djehuty smashed the staff down on the Prince's head and knocked him senseless[13].

5 Djehuty stuffed the stunned Prince into a bag. Then he dressed himself in the Prince's robes and spoke to the bodyguards. He told them that he had captured Djehuty and he wanted them to take the 200 donkeys and the 200 wine jars into Joppa.

13 The prince didn't have much sense to be knocked senseless. Fancy falling for a trick like that.

6 Djehuty told them that the Egyptian army had run away once they knew their general had been captured. Sure enough there wasn't an Egyptian soldier in sight. So the bodyguard set off back to the city. They led the 200 donkeys with the 200 jars up to the gates.

7 As soon as the donkeys were inside the city the Joppa soldiers started to smash the jars. But out of each jar leapt an Egyptian soldier, fully armed.

8 Djehuty threw off his prince disguise and slashed open the bag. He dragged out the real Prince and held a sword to his throat.

9 The soldiers of Joppa fell to their knees and surrendered. Djehuty raised the flag of Egypt over the city.

10 So Joppa was captured and Djehuty became a hero. He'd conquered the city and no one had been hurt.

Oh, all right … HARDLY anyone was hurt.

Of course the story is very similar to the Wooden Horse of Troy.

Is it true? Is it a legend? You decide…

Quick Egyptian quiz

Do you have a fair old brain (or even a pharaoh brain)? Or are you a mummy's boy? Test yourself with these quaint questions.

1 Pilgrims came to Egypt like holiday-makers to Blackpool. What miniature mummies did they buy as souvenirs? (Clue: did they have to kill these creatures nine times?)

2 Egyptian gods were often pictured with animal heads. Hapy had a baboon's head and Qebehsenuef had a falcon's. But Horemheb was buried with a rare god who had what sort of head? (Clue: flipping tortoise!)

3 The god Khnum created the first Egyptian people. What did he make them from? (Clue: they were earthy people.)

4 Farmers scattered corn on their fields. How did they trample the seed in so the birds couldn't eat it all? (Clue: they were seen and herd.)

5 Another way to keep birds off crops was to use scarecrows. These scarecrows were cleverer than modern ones as they could run around screaming! How?

6 The Egyptians made houses from bricks. The bricks were made from mud mixed with straw or something else. What? (Clue: not to be sniffed at.)

7 A weaver who took a day off work would be punished. How? (Clue: you can't beat it.)

8 Priests shaved off all their hair and eyebrows. Why? (Clue: not such a lousy idea.)

9 After reigning for 30 years a pharaoh would have to prove his strength. How? (Clue: it was a good idea in the long run.)

10 How many sides has an Egyptian pyramid?

Answers:

1 Mummified cats. The cats had their necks broken then were wrapped like a pharaoh's mummy. Pilgrims offered the cats to the gods. Vast cemeteries have been discovered with many thousands of these cat burials. It is likely that the animals were specially bred for this purpose. By 1900 hundreds of TONS of mummified cats had been shipped to Liverpool to be ground up and used as fertiliser.

Horrible Histories note: Some school books tell you the Egyptians mummified their cats because they loved their cute little Tiddles so much! Nice idea – load of rubbish.

2 A turtle. This was not a common statue in Egypt so Horemheb probably had to shell out a lot of money for it!

3 Mud. The early Egyptians called themselves 'black-landers' because they believed they were made from the dark, rich soil by the River Nile. Khnum, they said, breathed life into them and the mud became human beings. Muddy marvellous!

OOOH, LOOK AT HIM!

HIS NILE MUD BULGES IN ALL THE RIGHT WAYS

YEAH! NICE ONE KHNUM

4 With a herd of sheep, goats or pigs. These herds ran around the field and trampled in the grain. Don't try this at home.

5 Because the Egyptians used children as scarecrows. Nowadays we'd probably use traffic wardens because they are scarier than anything.

116

6 Animal droppings. Poo! Imagine if your house was made of mud mixed with animal droppings! Maybe it is! And imagine mixing it in those days before rubber gloves had been invented. They also burned animal droppings to make a fire.

7 He was beaten. Miss a day's work, weaver, and you get 50 lashes. And weaving was a tough job – you worked all day with your knees drawn up to your chest.

8 To keep free of lice. Everyone from pharaoh to peasant suffered from lice in their hair. Priests became slapheads (and slap-foreheads) to keep clean.

9 He had to run around his palace. Some historians believe that in the early days of Egypt, if the king failed the test he would be sacrificed. He was literally running for his life!

10 Two. An in-side and an out-side. (Oh, come on! This is a *Horrible Histories* book! What did you expect? A FAIR question?)

Cool Cleo

The last great Queen of Egypt was Cleopatra. The Greeks had conquered Egypt 250 years previously and she was the end of the line … the sticky end.

Cool Cleo facts

1 Cleo was probably not a beautiful woman. She had a long hooked nose, a thick neck and looked more like a man.

2 Cleo was clever. She spoke nine languages and was the first of her family to speak Egyptian.

3 The Egyptians treated her like a pharaoh even though she was from a Greek family and a woman. She worshipped the gods of Egypt.

4 Cleo took the throne when she was about 17 years old in 51 BC. She then married her brother, Ptolemy XIII, who was about 12.

5 The Roman general Pompey was in trouble with Julius Caesar and fled to Egypt. He landed in 48 BC … and was murdered as he stepped ashore. Little Ptolemy XIII watched.

6 Julius Caesar landed a few days later. Cleo had a long carpet rolled out for him. Cleo was wrapped in the carpet. Surprise! Surprise!

7 Ptolemy XIII ran away when he saw sister Cleo siding with the Romans. He drowned in the Nile as he fled. Cleo simply married brother Ptolemy XIV but her real love was Julius Caesar.

8 When Ptolemy XIV was no more use to her she had him poisoned. Thanks Sis. But Caesar was murdered in Rome.
9 Cleo married new Roman leader Mark Antony in 37 BC but they weren't a popular couple. Mark Antony was attacked by a Roman army and he blamed Cleo for his defeat.

10. To escape his anger she locked herself in her treasure house and sent a message that read 'Cleopatra is dead.'

What happened next is one of the most famous stories in history.

Antony heard Cleo was dead. He went to his room, crying that he would soon be with Cleopatra.

He told his servant Eros...

Antony had himself carried to her treasure house. Cleo was afraid to open the door in case the Romans rushed in, but she and her two serving women let down ropes from a window and pulled him up.

Cleopatra laid Antony on her bed but it was no good … he died.

Cleo locked the doors to her treasure house and refused to come out. When the Roman leader Octavian and his men arrived, Cleopatra refused to let them in. She talked with them through the locked door.

But Octavian was sneaky – he kept her talking while his men set up ladders and climbed through the window.

When Cleo saw the men she pulled out a dagger and tried to stab herself – she missed and was taken prisoner. Her children were taken prisoner too.

Octavian let Cleopatra arrange Antony's funeral. She buried him, then collapsed, sick with a broken heart.

And Cleopatra DID die. But how? Maybe not the way they tell you in the history books. There are TWO tales of her death…

The usual story – Cleo and the awful asp

Here is the history-book story…

a) Cleo wanted to kill herself, but Octavian had her watched.

b) One day he visited her and she flung herself at his feet and told him she wanted to live.

c) Cleo ordered a feast. A man arrived with a basket of figs. Octavian's guards checked the basket and found nothing wrong with it, so they let the man in.

IN FACT THERE IS A POISONOUS ASP SNAKE HIDDEN IN THE BASKET. BUT WHAT DOES MY QUEEN WANT WITH A POISONOUS SNAKE?

DON'T ASP ME THAT!

d) After she had eaten, Cleopatra wrote a letter to Octavian. It said…

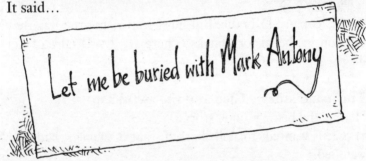

Let me be buried with Mark Antony

Then she pressed the asp to her arm.

JUST ONE BITE AND I'LL BE OUT LIKE A LIGHT

Octavian sent messengers to stop her killing herself. They came too late. They found her dead on her golden bed, with her maid Iras dying at her feet. Her other maid, Charmion, was putting Cleo's crown on her head. And she soon fell over dead too.

e) Two pricks were found on Cleopatra's arm, and it was believed that she had allowed herself to be bitten by an asp.

She was buried with Mark Antony as she had asked.

We don't know what happened to the asp.

You get the picture. Maybe you've heard the story. It is told in the play by William Shakespeare, *Antony and Cleopatra*.

It's one of the most famous love stories in history … but is it true?

Maybe all the history books got it wrong![14]

---

14 This is a *Horrible Histories* book, of course. We swear we will stab ourselves in the stomach with a rusty banana if we get it wrong.

The other story – Cleo and the murder mystery
No one wrote about Cleo's death when it happened. The story of the asp was written 100 years after she died.

Maybe Cleo DIDN'T kill herself. Here's why…

ROMANS KILL THEMSELVES – BUT EGYPTIANS DON'T. WE'D NEVER REST IN THE AFTERLIFE. AND, REMEMBER, I WORSHIPPED THE GODS OF EGYPT

WHY WOULD I SEND THE SUICIDE NOTE WHEN I WAS STILL ALIVE? IT DOESN'T MAKE SENSE

THE GUARDS DIDN'T FIND AN ASP WHEN THEY SEARCHED THE FIGS – A SNAKE UP TO 3 METRES LONG! MUST HAVE BEEN A HUGE BASKET OR BLIND GUARDS

ASP BITES TAKE ABOUT AN HOUR TO KILL YOU. THE GUARDS WERE THERE IN MINUTES. WHY DIDN'T THEY FIND US IN TIME AND SAVE US?

AND THE ASP WASN'T FOUND IN THE ROOM AFTER OUR DEATHS. DID IT EVER EXIST?

NO. IT WAS MURDER. AND THE MAIDS WERE KILLED BECAUSE THEY SAW WHAT HAPPENED

Quick question

Cleopatra and Julius Caesar had a son, Caesarion. Octavian was now emperor and he wanted Caesarion dead. He gave orders that the boy should be strangled. But who did the strangling?

a) The Emperor's cook, who was expert at strangling chickens for dinner.

b) Caesarion's teacher.

c) The Emperor's special assassin, who practised by strangling camels?

Answer: b) Yes, Caesarion was strangled by his own teacher. Would you believe it?

Epilogue

The Ancient Egyptians were amazing people. They lived in the Stone Age, when many humans elsewhere in the world did nothing but grunt and hunt.

They were led by clever and powerful pharaohs – maybe the cleverest people on Earth at that time. They managed to build massive pyramids then set off to conquer as much of the world as they wanted.

There was one thing that drove those phantastic pharaohs on – fear of death if they'd led a wicked life.

A pharaoh would tell you...

THERE IS NO SUCH THING AS DEATH

YOU COULD HAVE FOOLED ME!

They were sure that a person simply left this world and went on to another life.

If you had been a GOOD person then you went on to a better life.

One prayer was written in 1550 BC and it showed just how good you had to be. Would YOU be good enough? The prayer promised the gods...

126

1. PRAISE AM-KHAIBIT, I HAVE NEVER KILLED A MAN OR A WOMAN
2. PRAISE UTU-NESERT, I HAVE NEVER SWORN
3. PRAISE NEBA, I HAVE NEVER TOLD A LIE
4. PRAISE HER-F-HA-F, I HAVE NEVER MADE ANYONE WEEP
5. PRAISE BASTI, I HAVE NEVER EATEN ANY HEART
6. PRAISE TA-RETIU, I HAVE NEVER ATTACKED ANYONE
7. PRAISE KHEMIU, I HAVE NOT BROKEN THE LAW
8. PRAISE SHEP-KHERU, I HAVE NEVER LOST MY TEMPER
9. PRAISE SER-KHERU, I HAVE NEVER STIRRED UP TROUBLE
10. PRAISE AHI, I HAVE NEVER RAISED MY VOICE

How many would you score out of ten? If you can say yes to everything on the list then you can go to the good afterlife.

TEN OUT OF TEN!

ER-THAT'S A NUMBER THREE, I THINK, WAYNE

If you'd been a BAD person you went on to torment and misery. But at least your spirit lived on…

But worst of all was to have your body destroyed. Then your spirit would be homeless and that would be a disaster.

That's why the posh people went to so much trouble to make mummies and make thief-proof tombs.

They failed. Every tomb was robbed – many mummies were wrecked.

For all their brains the pharaohs forgot one important thing – how greedy and ruthless their poor peasants could be.

AWFUL EGYPTIANS

GRISLY QUIZ

Now find out if you're an
awful Egyptians expert!

EXTRAORDINARY ANCIENT EGYPT

How would you fare in the whacky world of ancient Egypt? Take this quick quiz and find out if you're clever enough to be worshipped as a fearful pharaoh or so stupid you'd be set to work as a slave.

1. How might Ancient Egyptians treat a nasty cut?
a) Strap a piece of fresh meat to it
b) Smear it with horse dung
c) Chop off the injured finger/arm/head

2. How did pharaoh Pepi II keep flies away from him?
a) He invented the first fly spray using cat urine
b) He had his slaves covered in honey so the flies would buzz off towards them
c) He ordered his army to kill all flies

3. How did ancient Egyptian embalmers remove the brain from dead pharaohs?
a) They stuck a hook up the nose and pulled the brain out through the nostrils
b) They sliced open the top of the head and removed the brain with a special spoon
c) They sucked it out through the ears using a straw

4. What does the pharaoh Ramesses' name mean?
a) 'Re has chosen him'
b) 'Re has finished him'
c) 'Re has sneezed on him'

5. The ancient Egyptians were crazy about cats. How did they mourn their mangy moggies when they died?

a) They wore black for a month
b) They sacrificed mice at a statue of the cat
c) They shaved off their eyebrows

6. What was the name of the ancient Egyptian book of prayers used to protect against evil spirits?
a) 101 Ways to Protect Against Evil Spirits
b) The Dangerous Book for Mummies
c) Book of the Dead

7. How were gruesome grave robbers punished?
a) They were impaled on a sharp stick
b) They were buried alive in the grave they robbed
c) They were beheaded with an axe

8. According to legend, how did Cleopatra, the last queen of Egypt, die?
a) She was strangled by a snake
b) She was bitten by a snake
c) She was murdered and fed to a snake

GROOVY GODS

The ancient Egyptian gods were a confusing crew – they took on all sorts of names and shapes and they were all in charge of different areas of life (and death). Some of the greatest and ghastliest gods introduce themselves below. Can you work out who's who?

1. Don't be fooled by my beetle-like body. I might roll around in poo (or roll poo around), but I'm actually the sun-god reborn, which makes me pretty powerful. (Or should that be poo-erful?)

2. I'm a cow-headed lady who loves a good time – the goddess of music, dance and drinking. So if you fancy grooving with the gods, pop round to my place for a bit of a party.

3. You might say I'm the unluckiest of the gods – murdered by my brother, chopped into pieces and scattered to the four winds. Luckily my wife Isis managed to find most bits of me and stick me back together again, but I'm a bit green from the experience.

4. I might look like a monkey (or maybe a frog), but you don't want to monkey around with me – I'm the king of the gods, an all-powerful almighty.

5. If you fancy a spot of bother I'm the god to see – the lord of chaos and evil. Trouble is my middle name. If you want to know how murderous I am, just ask my brother Osiris…

6. I hold the power of (after)life and death in my hands. Come and see me and we'll have a good heart to heart… Actually I'll put your heart on my scales and decide if it's weighed down with wickedness or as light as a feather.

7. I'm the school swot in the world of the gods – lord of wisdom and writing. I might look like a baboon, but I'm no boob…

8. You might have seen pictures of me – I'm the one with the head of a hawk wearing a funny hat. Despite my dubious dress sense, I'm a powerful god, in charge of the king and kids.

a) Osiris, b) Anubis, c) Seth, d) Hathor, e) Horus, f) Thoth, g) Khepri, h) Amun

EGYPTIAN FACT OR FICTION

While the rest of the world was wandering around in animal skins and using basic stone tools, our Egyptian friends were reading, writing and ruling an awesome civilization. Can you work out which of the following facts about these ancient experts are true and which are just mad myths?

1. The first workers to go on strike were ancient Egyptian workers.

2. The ancient Egyptians counted how many they had killed after a battle by chopping off the heads of their dead enemies.

3. Scissors were invented by the ancient Egyptians.

4. Ancient Egyptian doctors believed they could cure toothache by placing a dead mouse in the patient's mouth.

5. Some of the Kush kings from Sudan had their rotten relatives buried with them when they died.

6. The Egyptians were the first people to make toffee apples.

7. It took around 25,000 slaves five years to build just one pyramid.

8. The best ancient Egyptian soldiers weren't sent to fight wars, they were used to guard the pharaoh's palace.

BARMY EMBALMING

Below is a page from the secret diary of an Egyptian embalmer. Unfortunately it's so very ancient that some of the words have faded away. Fill in the gaps to make sense of the mad method of mummification.

Dear Diary,

Well we finally finished mummifying the old pharaoh yesterday, so he's good and ready for the 1)_____. It's a disgusting job being an embalmer, I can tell you. To begin with, he was pretty stinky, so we took him to a special tent to blow away the fumes. When he was a bit less pongy we started work. First we pulled out his 2)_____ (by way of his nose) and packed the empty space with 3)_____ to stop it rotting. Next we ripped out his liver, stomach, intestines and lungs. Sounds brutal, but don't worry, we stored them carefully in 4)_____ in case he needs them later. We left the 5)_____ where it was, of course. He'll be wanting that. After the body had been properly pickled in salt, it was looking a bit shrivelled and empty, so we stuffed it with 6)_____ to plump it up a bit. He looked more like his old self then, so we wrapped him in 7)_____. All that was left to do was to pop him in his 8)_____ and wish him bon voyage. Hope he makes it to the next world – he was a pretty nice fellow (as pharaohs go).

a) canopic jars, b) brain, c) linen, d) sarcophagus, e) natron, f) heart, g) afterlife, h) bandages

PHASCINATING PHARAOH PHACTS

The kings of Egypt ruled for nearly 3,000 years, so the history books are filled with facts about pharaohs. Some were cruel and some were clueless. Some lived long and prospered and others died dastardly deaths at the hands of assassins. Here are some curious questions about the most famous of these ruthless rulers…

1. Where did Pharaoh Khufu build his pyramid? (Clue: He was a greedy geezer.)

2. What was stuffed up Ramesses II's nose when he was being mummified? (Clue: He must have sneezed all the way to the afterlife.)

3. How did Pharaoh Amenemhet's tomb-makers try to stop grave robbers pillaging his pyramid? (Clue: You'll be amazed.)

4. What did the female pharaoh Hatshepsut wear to make her look more like a man? (Clue: It was a hairy disguise.)

5. How did Ramesses III punish the judges who went to parties with the people who plotted to kill him? (Clue: They didn't get a fair hearing!)

6. What is Pharaoh Pepi II most famous for? (Clue: Long live the king!)

7. Who did Amenhotep III take as his wife? (Clue: Keep it in the family.)

8. What did Pharaoh Narmer do to his enemies? (Clue: He showed them who was head honcho.)

Extraordinary Ancient Egypt
1a; 2b; 3a; 4b; 5c; 6c; 7a; 8b

Groovy Gods
1g; 2d; 3a; 4h; 5c; 6b; 7f; 8e

Egyptian Fact or Fiction
1. TRUE. Ancient Egyptian workers went on strike because they weren't paid on time. And they weren't even holding out for cash – they were paid in bags of corn!
2. FALSE. The awful Egyptians hacked off the HANDS of their enemies so they knew how many they had killed.
3. TRUE. Basic scissors have been found in ancient Egyptian ruins. They weren't particularly good because they were made from a single piece of metal (it was the ruthless Romans who thought it would be a better idea to have two separate blades).
4. TRUE. This probably didn't work, but at least it gave the sufferer something to suck on.
5. TRUE. But no one knows for sure why or how they were killed.
6. FALSE. They didn't invent toffee apples, but the ancient Egyptians were the first people to make marshmallows, from the roots of – yes, you guessed it – the marshmallow plant!
7. FALSE. The men who built the pyramids weren't slaves – they were paid workers. Aha – a trick question! Mean. It still took 25,000 of them five years to build one, though…
8. TRUE. This might explain why the Egyptians were often beaten in battle…

Barmy Embalming
1g; 2b; 3e; 4a; 5f; 6c; 7h; 8d

Phascinating Pharaoh Phacts
1. At Giza. It's the largest pyramid in Egypt.
2. The embalmers stuffed peppercorns up his nose to give it its shape back.
3. He built his pyramid as a maze of twisting tunnels and dead ends.
4. She would often wear a weird beard. I don't suppose anyone was fooled...
5. He had their ears cut off.
6. He had the longest reign of any ancient Egyptian pharaoh.
7. He married his own daughter, Satamum. But that wasn't as bad as Ramesses II, who married three of his own daughters!
8. He hacked off their heads.

INTERESTING INDEX

Where will you find 'rotten bodies', 'energetic elephants' and 'women with beards' in an index? In a Horrible Histories book, of course!

afterlife 5, 12, 14, 40–1, 44, 47, 50–1, 56, 76, 79, 124, 127

Akhenaten (pharaoh) 56

Alexander the Great (king of Macedonia) 8

Amenemhet (pharaoh) 76–9

Amenhotep II (pharaoh) 80, 82–3

Amenhotep III (pharaoh) 107

Amun (god) 84

Antony, Mark (Roman leader) 119–23

Anubis (god) 55, 85

archaeologists 57–9, 64

army, awful 107, 13

Ashurbanipal (king of Assyria) 8

Ay (Tutankhamun's uncle) 29, 73

beards
    on women 21
    wooden 106

bits, naughty 105, 109

bodies
    dead 53
    destroyed 128
    rotten 5, 44

    smashed open 82
    smelling 18
    stealing 76

Bonaparte, Napoleon (French emperor) 36–7

Book of the Dead 48–9, 51, 66

brick-makers 100

British Museum 48, 52, 65–6

Caesarion (Cleopatra's son) 125

camels, taming 102

canopic jars (containers for body bits) 12, 44

Carnarvon, Lord (British earl) 58, 64–6

Carter, Howard (British archaeologist) 58, 67

carvings 21–2

Cleopatra (Egyptian queen) 9, 31, 118–25

copper 12, 100

corn 106, 114

crime, cruel 71–83

Djhuty (Egyptian general) 110, 13

Djoser (pharaoh) 7, 12–13
doctors, disgusting 96
donkeys, deceptive 110–12

elephants, energetic 23, 27, 31, 43
embalmers (mummy-makers) 45, 47, 50

famine, foul 73
farm-workers 100
fishermen 101
flies 16
furnace-workers 101

grave robbers 8, 56–63, 75–9, 81–2, 128
Greeks, groovy 9, 31, 95, 104, 118
guts 12, 13, 104

Hathor (goddess) 85–6
Hatshepsut (pharaoh) 20–2
heart, weighing of the 51, 87
Hebrews (Jews) 26
Herodotus (Greek historian) 32–3
Hippocrates (Greek doctor) 95
Hittites, horrid (Egypt's enemies) 23–6,
31, 107
Hor Aha (pharaoh) 28, 30
horses 25, 40–1, 109
Horus (god) 55, 85–6, 88, 93
Hyksos (Asian tribe) 8, 19, 22

impaling, painful 63, 74
ink, making own 102
Isis (goddess) 86

Julius Caesar (Roman ruler) 120–1

Ka (spirit) 52–5, 128
Kadesh (Hittite city) 23˜5
Karnak Temple 103

Khepri (god) 86, 91
Khnum (god) 86, 114, 116
Khonsu (god) 105
Khufu (pharaoh) 14
Kush, crazy (Egypt's neighbour) 39–43

Loret, Victor (French historian) 80–2

Menkaure (pharaoh) 69–70
Mentuhotep (pharaoh) 17–18
messengers 101, 109–10
Moses (Hebrew leader) 26–7
mummies
    burning 79
    curse of 6, 45, 49, 51, 58, 64–9
    exposed 82
    feeding 54–5
    grinning 81
    mad 5, 20, 44–59
    main man of 85
    making 12, 44–7, 128
    miniature 114, 116
    neat 80
    old as 7

Narmer (pharaoh) 11–12
Nile (river) 7, 10, 72–3, 86, 92, 116, 118
Nubians, nasty (Egypt's neighbours) 18,
83, 107
Nut (goddess) 87, 90

Octavian (Roman leader) 120–3, 125
Osiris (god) 87

peasants, poor 10, 48, 70, 92, 117, 128
pens 102
Pepi II (pharaoh) 15–17
Persians, powerful 8
Petrie, Flinders (British historian) 75

pets 5, 31
pharaohs 7-8, 38, 44
    cruel 75-6, 81
    graveyard of 52
    phunny 10-31, 85, 92, 103, 105-6
    powerful 46, 50, 57-9, 115, 117-18, 126
    top ten 10-25
    truth about 63, 67, 69-70
potters 100
priests
    lousy 115, 117
    wearing skins 103, 106
    women as 105
pygmies (dwarves) 15-16
pyramids 7, 14, 77
    biggest 14
    perplexing 92, 115, 126
    potty 32-43

Ramesses II (pharaoh) 23-4, 26, 31
Ramesses III (pharaoh) 71-2, 106
Ramesses IV (pharaoh) 50
Re (god) 84
reeds 27, 100, 102
religion, rotten 84-92
Romans, rotten 9, 118-20, 124

sacrifices
    animal 103-4
    human 39-40, 63, 81, 83, 117
    savage 52-5, 84
scarecrows, children as 115-16
scribes, super 102-6
Senusret III (pharaoh) 18-19
servants, dead 5-6
Seth (god) 87-8
Shakespeare, William (English
playwright) 121
Shepherd of the Royal Backside 96

skulls 20, 44, 81
slaves 10, 26-7, 32-3
    honey-covered 16
    in afterlife 40
Sneferu (pharaoh) 29
soldiers 105, 107-9
Sphinx (stone statue) 36-8
statues 54, 105, 116

Tao (pharaoh) 19-20
taxes, not paying 102
thieves 7-4, 8, 56-63, 75-9, 81-2, 128
Thoth (god) 22, 84, 87
tombs, deadly dome 42-3
toothache, cures for 93-5
tradesmen, top ten 99-101
Tutankhamun (pharaoh) 28-9, 56, 60-7
Tuthmosis III (pharaoh) 22-3, 110

Valley of the Kings 52, 60, 80

washermen, filth-eating 101
weavers 100, 115, 117
Winlock, Herbert (American historian) 17
women
    with beards 21
    drinking beer 104
    as priests 105
workers, woeful 99-106
writing 7, 102

Terry Deary was born at a very early age, so long ago he can't remember. But his mother, who was there at the time, says he was born in Sunderland, north-east England, in 1946 – so it's not true that he writes all *Horrible Histories* from memory. At school he was a horrible child only interested in playing football and giving teachers a hard time. His history lessons were so boring and so badly taught, that he learned to loathe the subject. *Horrible Histories* is his revenge.

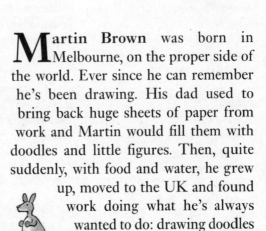

Martin Brown was born in Melbourne, on the proper side of the world. Ever since he can remember he's been drawing. His dad used to bring back huge sheets of paper from work and Martin would fill them with doodles and little figures. Then, quite suddenly, with food and water, he grew up, moved to the UK and found work doing what he's always wanted to do: drawing doodles and little figures.